To:
My Dear Friend
Brent P.

Love you
BSMW

Princess Butter Cup
5/5/17

WRITING MY WRONGS

WRITING MY WRONGS

Life, Death,
and Redemption
in an American Prison

SHAKA SENGHOR

CONVERGENT
BOOKS · NEW YORK

Copyright © 2013, 2016 by Drop a Gem Publishing, LLC

All rights reserved.
Published in the United States by Convergent Books,
an imprint of the Crown Publishing Group,
a division of Penguin Random House LLC, New York.
www.crownpublishing.com

CONVERGENT BOOKS and its open book colophon
are registered trademarks of Penguin Random House LLC.

Originally published by Drop a Gem Publishing, LLC,
in different form, in 2013. Selected material originally appeared
on the author's blog at medium.com/@shakasenghor.

Library of Congress Cataloging-in-Publication Data is available
upon request.

ISBN 978-1-101-90729-0
eBook ISBN 978-1-101-90730-6

PRINTED IN THE UNITED STATES OF AMERICA

Jacket design by Christopher Brand
Jacket photograph by Northbound Films

10 9 8 7 6 5

First Revised Edition

To Ebony, thank you for everything you do to support
my dream and vision. You are my rock, and I deeply appreciate
you for being the rare jewel of a woman that you are.
You truly are my everything, and it's an honor to be sharing
this journey with you.

To my children Lakeisha Todd, James Angelo White II, and
Sekou Senghor, I love you more than words can express.

To my parents James and Marie White and Ronald (RIP) and
Arlene Howard, thank you for your love and support.

To my brothers on lockdown who are working hard
to make a difference and transform their lives,
you inspire and motivate me.

To the victims of crimes throughout the world,
your pain will never be forgotten.

The unexamined life is not worth living.

—Socrates, Plato's *Apology*

FOREWORD

On July 1, 2012, the MIT Media Lab announced that we would be creating an Innovators Guild—a team of scholars, executives, and designers that would go to communities around the world using the power of innovation to help people. Our first focus was Detroit.

Three weeks later the Knight Foundation, which was funding our trip, organized a meeting with the city's community leaders. We gave presentations about MIT and the Media Lab and about how we had come to Detroit to explore how we could create innovative solutions to long-standing problems.

Then, during the Q&A, a tough-looking Black man with dreadlocks stood up. "Many well-meaning people come to Detroit with a missionary mentality," he said. "Then they get discouraged when they realize just how tough our problems are. If you want to make a real impact, you have to go out among the people in the communities and not buy into the romanticized view of Detroit based on midtown and downtown." Although there were other comments expressing skepticism toward our efforts, this one stood out. We realized we were staring reality in the face.

After the meeting, the man introduced himself as Shaka. He said that if we were willing he would show us the real Detroit. We immediately accepted the offer. On our next trip, we avoided downtown altogether and went straight to Brightmoor on Detroit's West Side, a neighborhood full of burned-out, vacant homes and liquor stores fronted with bulletproof glass. Shaka told us stories that had none of the romance, but they were true.

We quickly realized that we couldn't just fly in, do good, and go home. We needed to introduce ourselves to the community, learn about the people who lived there, and build trust. If we wanted to have a positive impact on Detroit, we had to be there for the long haul.

In the following weeks, my team from the Media Lab and creatives from the design firm IDEO flew to Detroit, working with Shaka and others to come up with a plan for how we might be able to join the community and work together. We then invited Shaka and the Detroit team to the MIT Media Lab to meet students and faculty and see and learn about what we do. Bonds began forming between the Lab and the Detroiters.

In October, we all converged on Detroit, setting up a base at the headquarters of OmniCorpDetroit, a vital local organization. We were an eclectic group of community leaders, chief innovation officers, students, and designers. Each team started working on projects ranging from solving the streetlight issue to urban farming. Shaka emerged as our natural leader, keeping the energy high and the teams working together.

By the end of an insanely productive three days, I had a plan. I would make Shaka an MIT Media Lab Fellow. He'd be our man in Detroit—our connection to the incredibly important world he represents. Since then, Shaka and the Media Lab team have started to work together extensively, and Shaka continues to inspire and challenge us.

In December, Shaka e-mailed me that he had a rough draft of

his memoirs and asked if I was interested in reading it. I read the entire book in two sittings. Shaka is, among his other talents, an amazing storyteller. The book is funny and moving and astute, and by the end I felt as if I had been the one convicted of murder, as if I'd spent seven years in the hole, and gone through the dramatic transformation from angry, scared young boy to enlightened teacher and leader.

And by the end, I could begin to see how a generation of bright children full of promise are channeled into a system that sees them as little more than felons-in-waiting. Yet again, Shaka has inspired me to help right the wrongs, in this instance by helping him write the wrongs.

The book may be about Shaka's past, but it points to a future in which we all take the next step to build a more just society.

Joi Ito
Director, MIT Media Lab
January 2013

WRITING MY WRONGS

PROLOGUE

OAKS CORRECTIONAL FACILITY
Manistee, Michigan
2001

I stared at the mirror, watching the tears roll slowly down my face, each drop carrying the pain of my childhood. I was on my second year of a four-and-a-half-year stint in solitary confinement. It was my deepest moment of reflection, a sacred moment of clarity when I came face-to-face with true forgiveness.

I walked over to the steel sink-toilet combo that was next to my cell door. The cell was spartan in appearance, with a brick slab and a plastic green mattress for a bed. The mirror was a sheet of polished steel, because in prison they didn't allow real mirrors.

I stared at the battle-scarred image in front of me and knew I needed to begin the long, tedious process of making peace with my past. I opened up deep wounds that had been stuffed with the gauze of anger and self-hatred. I forgave all of the people who had

1

teased me in my childhood, making fun of my jack-o'-lantern-sized head by calling me Pumpkin. I forgave everyone who had made fun of my gap-toothed smile. I ran my hands through my long dreadlocks and forgave everyone who ever called me nappy-headed, making me feel insecure about the crown my Creator had bestowed upon me. The words from my past ricocheted around in my mind like errant bullets, hurting no less now than they had back then.

I forgave my mother for all of the ass whoppings she gave me, remembering the fire of the belt cutting into my tender flesh. I forgave her for all of the moments she wasn't there when I needed her. I forgave the guy who shot me when I was seventeen and made me feel like I had to carry a gun. I forgave my siblings and homies for abandoning me at the lowest point in my life.

The levees broke, and I began sobbing harder than I ever had before. But I could also feel a deep, abiding peace rushing over the toxic hatred from my past.

People had told me about the healing power of forgiveness, but it had taken me until now to understand that forgiveness wasn't only about letting other people off the hook. It was about me. I had to free myself from the anger, fear, and hurt of my past. I had to forgive the people I hated. Most important, I had to forgive myself.

This was one of the hardest things I had ever done, because I didn't feel I was worthy of forgiveness. I was a murderer. Guilt from the destruction and disappointment I had caused clung to me like a sweaty T-shirt, but I knew in my heart that if I wanted to make things right with others, I had to make them right with myself. In order to feel like I was capable of forgiving them, I had to release myself from the burden of all the hurt I had brought into the world.

James Allen's book *As a Man Thinketh* had helped me to see that I was responsible for my thoughts and the feelings that they produced. It didn't matter what other people had done to me; ultimately, I was responsible for my anger, and for the actions that I took in response to it.

All of which brought me to this moment, staring at a broken man's face in the scratched steel mirror of Cell 211, in the solitary confinement wing of a correctional facility in western Michigan. It was the beginning of a journey that would culminate eight years later, when I wrote a letter to the man I had killed.

By then, I was finishing up a therapy course for violent offenders and preparing to see the parole board for the second time, to make the case for my release. But I realized that if I wanted to move forward with my life, there was one more thing I needed to do. I needed to come to terms with the man I had taken out of this world. (Out of respect to my victim's family and their privacy, I have changed his name.)

Dear Mr. Clarke

I am writing this letter to share with you what has been on my mind and heart for several years now. For the last few nights, I have stayed awake writing this letter in my head, and each time, I found myself mentally balling up the pages because I couldn't find the right words to convey how deeply sorry I am for causing your death. Somehow, no matter what words I use, saying I am sorry for robbing you and your family of your life seems too small of a gesture.

Every time I think back to that night, I find myself asking the question, "Why didn't I just walk away?" When I finally found the answer, I understood for the first time the true meaning of the words "weakness" and "strength." See, all my life, I had confused their meaning. I thought walking away from an argument would make me appear weak and make me a loser. But in reality, it takes strength to walk away from conflict. Back then, I didn't have that strength. I was afraid, and I allowed my fears to dictate my actions. Sixteen months prior to the night I shot you, I too was shot in a similar incident. I survived, but I became consumed by fear and paranoia. I thought it could happen again at any given moment. I became desperately angry, because anger was the only emotion that could conceal the fear.

When you and I encountered each other, I was already programmed to kill. I had convinced myself that it was better to shoot than to be shot; that the handgun in my pocket was the only thing that could protect me. In my mind, it was easier to shoot than to walk away, and I have spent the last 17 years learning just how wrong I was.

For years, I blamed you for making me mad enough to shoot you. Now I realize that no one can make me feel anything I don't want to feel. I blamed your death on the fact that we were both intoxicated, but now I recognize that the instinct to shoot anyone I perceived as a threat had been planted long before we met. Even though I pled guilty in court, I blamed everything and everyone but myself. Pleading guilty was easy because I knew I had violated the law, but it didn't mean I was taking full responsibility for having caused your death.

It wasn't until I was ten years into serving my sentence that I began seeing things differently. My healing started when I learned to begin forgiving myself for the wrongs I had committed. However the real change started a year later, when my eleven-year-old son sent me a letter that said he had found out the real reason I was in prison. Knowing my son would see me as a murderer made me face up to the fact that my thinking and my choices had caused your death and led to me losing my freedom.

Today, when I look back, I wish I could change the past. I

wish I could restore your life so that your children could have known the safety and security of having their father in the house. I wish I could bring you back to life so that your wife could enjoy the presence of her husband and your parents could see you reaching for your dreams.

I'm sorry. Please forgive me.

I know that saying I'm sorry can never restore your life. But I believe in the power of atonement, and I have taken responsibility for my actions by dedicating my life and talents to making amends for the pain I have brought into this world. For the last five years, I have been actively involved with anti-violence organizations that work with at-risk youth. I have used my talent as a writer to share my story—our story—so that others may learn from it and make better choices with their own lives. It doesn't change what I did, but I want you to know that your life was not, and will not be, in vain.

I first learned about the power of forgiveness from your godmother, Mrs. Weaver, who started writing me five years into my sentence. She wanted to know what had happened that night—why I had shot and killed you. It's one of the hardest questions I've ever had to answer, but I knew that I owed your family closure. I told Mrs. Weaver about our dispute, leaving out the fact that it was started by a drug transaction because I didn't feel that it was necessary for them to be exposed to that part of your life. I told her that you didn't deserve it; that I wished more than anything else in the world that I could change what happened on that night.

She wrote back two weeks later. She said that she forgave me and encouraged me to seek God's forgiveness, and I took her words to heart. It would be five long years before I reached the point when I could truly forgive myself. But I did, and today, I can't help but wonder if your godmother's care was the first real step in my transformation.

I know that even though I have evolved and taken the necessary steps to right my wrongs, I still have a lot of work to do. But each day I am blessed with life, I know that I now have the will to live with meaning and purpose.

Sincerely,
Shaka

PART ONE

1

The sound of sirens burst through the quiet morning air, startling me awake. I crawled from beneath the scratchy wool blanket, rose to my feet, and approached the door to my cell, where a chubby roach was navigating its way across the cold, gray bars. I hollered down the tier, trying to figure out what was going on.

"Yo, Satan, what the fuck they hit the siren for?" I asked, wiping the crust from the corner of my eyes.

Gigolo, whom everyone called Satan, was one of the few cats I spoke to on a regular basis. In jail, friendliness was frowned upon, so I didn't talk to anyone unless we had something in common beyond being locked up. Gigolo and I were from different cities, but we had grown up in similar environments and had formed a bond during the time I'd been in county jail.

"I don't know, homie," Gigolo yelled back from a few cells down. "You know how they do around here. They probably hate that they ass can't get no sleep, so they fucking with us." A few other inmates laughed.

Gigolo's statement expressed the sentiment of most of the cats on lockdown. We had come to believe that the deputies would do anything they could to make our stay as unbearable as possible. They would bang their keys on the bars, turn the bright lights on in the middle of the night, and hold loud conversations during hours when we were trying to sleep. But if they had intended for this to intimidate us, it didn't work. Most of us had come from environments where disrespect, violence, and abuse were the norm. We were used to it—and besides, you can't change a person for the better by treating him or her like an animal. The way I see it, you get out of people what you put into them, so the officers were only making their jobs harder.

Another inmate called from farther down the tier. "They might be coming to get y'all and take y'all to different county jails," he yelled.

"Come get us for what?" Gigolo asked, a bit irritated.

"Man, they take that escape shit serious. Ain't nobody tried to pull off that shit y'all just tried," he said, alluding to the escape attempt that had landed Gigolo and me in the hole.

Another voice hollered from the end of the tier. "Bitch ass nigga, mind your business 'cause you speaking on shit you don't even know about. You working with the police or something, saying some shit like that? You don't know if them brothers tried to escape or not. You trying to get niggas indicted around this bitch?" Everyone burst into laughter.

"Man, I was just saying," the first inmate stammered.

"That's the problem now, so shut the fuck up!" This led to more laughter.

I sat on the corner of my bunk and listened to the inmates argue back and forth as the sirens continued to blare. It felt odd, listening to two strangers speak with so much authority about something I had been accused of doing. It had been a week since Gigolo, Gee, White Boy, Jabo, and I were placed in the hole and charged with attempting to escape from the sixth floor of the Wayne County Jail. With no evidence other than a confidential statement made by another inmate, we were found guilty and sentenced to fifteen days in solitary confinement.

Two days after being thrown in the hole, we were each called out by an officer from the Internal Affairs Division. He threatened us with lengthy sentences and then promised us the world if we snitched on one another. One by one, we refused to answer any questions regarding the escape attempt, and the matter was dropped as far as Internal Affairs was concerned. But the Wayne County hearing officer, who was basically an internal, autonomous judge and jury, found us guilty. It was an irony that vexed us to no end. In jail and in prison, when a confidential informant makes a statement against an inmate, it's enough to find him or her guilty of any charge. But when we have witnesses who are capable of exonerating us, their testimony is no good.

The Wayne County Sherriff's Office had suffered great embarrassment from our almost-successful escape attempt, but it turned out that the sirens had been sounded for a much more sinister occasion.

After half an hour of blaring, the siren suddenly cut off, leaving an eerie silence in its wake. Within moments, we could hear keys jingling and the urgent crackling of deputies' radios. For us, those noises would become the soundtrack of chaos.

A team of deputies, better known as the goon squad, burst through the door of our tier and began snatching us out of our cells, one at a time. The officers wore an assortment of expressions: astonished, sad, angry. The officer who came to remove me was one of the few we all considered cool. Unlike most guards, who thought it was their personal duty to add to our misery, he understood that for the most part we were all miserable, and he would come to work cracking jokes and talking shit to lighten the mood. Some days, he would leave the entrance door to our tier cracked and turn on the radio to FM 98, Detroit's hip-hop and R & B station. It was a small gesture, but it went a long way to break up the monotony of the hole.

But today was different. When he ordered me to step out of my cell, he had a look of total disbelief on his face. I could sense that something was seriously wrong, so I asked him what was going on. He hesitated before he spoke.

"Somebody shot and killed Sergeant Dickerson," he responded solemnly.

"Do they think we had something to do with it?" I asked, trying to fit the pieces of the puzzle together.

"No," he whispered as another officer approached with handcuffs. "They're just taking precautions."

It wasn't until later that we would find out what had happened, and when we did, we were as astounded as the officers. By the administration's account, an inmate had attempted to escape by smuggling a gun into the county jail. Allegedly, he had thrown a handmade rope out of the window and gotten someone on the street below to tie a gun to it. Then, later that day, he was on his way to court when he pulled out the gun in an attempt to liberate himself. A scuffle ensued, and when the dust settled, Officer Dickerson lay dead.

I had been at Wayne County Jail for six weeks, following my arrest and conviction for second-degree murder. In those six weeks, I had witnessed everything from rape and robbery to murder, and this was one more reminder that inmates had no shortage of creativity when it came to inflicting harm on other men. Little did I know, this was just beginning my education in the true meaning of violence.

2

Six weeks earlier I was sitting in a dingy cell at the police head-quarters on Beaubien. It was my second arrest as a young adult, and by far the most serious in my short career as a street hustler. The days of going to the precinct or youth home only to be let right back out were over. This wasn't a drug rap or assault charge—the kind of thing I was used to getting into. This time, it was murder.

One month after my nineteenth birthday, I had officially grad-uated to the big leagues. There would be no more slaps on the wrist or warnings from an irate judge, no bailouts from a counselor who saw potential in me. If I lost this one, it could cost me the rest of my life in prison, but that was a reality that my young mind wasn't ready to accept.

The sound of bars rattling made me snap to attention. I removed the shirt that had been covering my head, and a light-skinned officer was standing at the cell bars with a no-nonsense expression on his face.

"Get up and get dressed," he barked. "You're being transferred to the county jail." He turned and walked down the tier, repeating the same order to a handful of other unfortunate souls.

"Wayne County Jail": three words every hustler and street thug in Detroit feared hearing. The stories of violence, corruption, and desperation in WCJ were legendary. The seven-story building on St. Antoine looked inconspicuous enough, but inside, the law of the jungle prevailed. In the early eighties, during the heyday of Young Boys Incorporated—one of Detroit's first major drug rings—the jail's reputation for violence skyrocketed. Among the tiers named after characters from the *Transformers* TV show, few inmates could count themselves safe from unprovoked attacks, mostly from other inmates. From robberies to beatings and rape, anyone entering was considered fair game.

I pulled myself up from the small, cramped bunk, slipped into my shoes, and walked over to the bars. I looked out onto the dusty tier as I slipped on the shirt I had been wearing for the last three days. I smelled like I had been sleeping in a garbage Dumpster.

The sound of clanking metal shot down the hall as officers opened and shut the cells of other inmates, herding the guys down the tier and into a holding cell, in preparation for their transfer to the county jail.

Soon, it was my turn. The officer opened my cell, and I shuffled down the hallway slowly, holding up my shorts and doing my best not to lose my shoes. (They had taken my belt and shoelaces when I entered the precinct—their way of making sure we didn't hang ourselves or choke someone else.) When I reached the intake desk, they returned my shoelaces, belt, and the knot of money that had been in my pocket when they arrested me. The thick wad of hundred- and twenty-dollar bills was a reminder of the city streets I had left behind, and the weight of it in my hand made a current of excitement shoot through my body. But the feeling soon evaporated as I realized I might never see the streets of Detroit again.

At the end of the tier, an officer pushed me inside the holding pen, where a dozen or so other inmates were waiting. Most of them were in their early to mid-twenties, and from the looks on their faces, it was clear that they were thinking the same thing I was thinking. How had our lives come to this? And what would we find waiting for us on the other side?

As I stood there in cuffs, my thoughts wandered back to my childhood. I thought about the first time my mother asked me what I wanted to be when I grew up. I had told her that I wanted to be a doctor. I wanted to help people get better, to mend their broken bones. I wanted to be the kind of doctor who gave children balloons and lollipops anytime they had to get a shot.

But the image of me with a white coat and a stethoscope faded as my thoughts returned to the present. I stood with my back against the wall of the dingy pen, wondering if there might still be a way out of this. All I needed was one more shot at freedom, one more chance to turn my life around.

It wasn't the first time I had told myself that. There was the time I was charged with felonious assault and drug possession and sent to the Wayne County Youth Home. I promised my father that I would turn my life around when I got out, and for a few months, I did. I went off to Job Corps in Prestonsburg, Kentucky, got my GED, and started working as a carpenter. But I hadn't relinquished my old ways. The entire time I was there, I sold six-dollar joints and ran a loan-sharking ring. When I was caught, I was sent back home on the next Greyhound, to my father's great disappointment.

Then there was the case I had just beaten in Monroe County.

I had been driving back from one of my drug-selling trips to Ohio with a car full of cash and a trunk full of guns when a policeman pulled us over and arrested us for receiving and concealing stolen property. After the arrest, I told myself that this was it. I was tired of the streets and all that came with them. But as soon as we beat the case and returned to Detroit, it was business as usual.

That was the routine. As long as there was a threat to my freedom, I acted like I was ready to change, but the moment I got free, I didn't care anymore. It would take ten years and a lot misfortune for me to understand that real change comes only when you are completely and thoroughly disgusted with your actions and the consequences that they produce. As the Honorable Elijah Muhammad once said, "One hundred percent dissatisfaction brings about one hundred percent change." And in 1991, I was only about 40 percent dissatisfied.

I loved living in the streets. I loved the fast money, fast cars, and fast women. Above all, I loved the reputation I had earned in the 'hood. People knew me as a crazy motherfucker who would shoot as soon as I detected the slightest threat to me and my crew. When I drove or walked around the 'hood, people acknowledged me out of fear or respect, and that was the greatest feeling in the world. It was the one thing that made me feel like I was somebody, like I had power, like I had control over my life. I was the embodiment of what noted Black psychologist Amos Wilson argued: that the young Black male has perfected the art of being the best at being the worst.

Back in the holding pen, I was pulled out of my train of thought by the feeling that I was being watched. Sure enough, when I looked up, a tall, slim guy was staring at me. I returned his stare, then went over to ask if he had a problem. That's what you did in the 'hood, jail, and the prison yard. If you and another male exchanged glances, you'd better be up to the challenge, or you would be considered weak. And in our world, the weak became prey.

When I walked up to the guy, a smile creased his face, and he told me he remembered me from over on a street named Savannah, where my sister had lived back in the day. His name was Jimmy, but I barely recognized him because he had grown several inches since I had last seen him. We kicked it about the old neighborhood for a minute, then he told me that he had overheard the officers talking about my charges. They were disturbed that such a violent act could have been committed by such a young kid.

Some of the older brothers nearby began to sidle up, listening to snippets of our conversation. They were intrigued by my youthfulness and the callous manner in which I boasted about how I was going to beat a murder rap. In a twisted way, all of this attention made me feel like a celebrity.

This kind of thinking is common among marginalized Black and Latino males. In the 'hood, the villain is the hero, the guy people look up to. So we hang out in front of liquor stores with plastic bags in our boxers and semiautomatics tucked into our waistbands, living out our version of the American dream.

Jimmy and I continued to talk about the old days until two deputies came and took us away. They herded us out of the building and into a white Wayne County Sheriff's van along with eight other inmates. On the drive to the jail, most of us grew quiet and looked down at the van's metal floor. We all felt the same nervous energy, but we kept it concealed under the stoic masks we had worn standing on the corners in our respective 'hoods. From the streets of Detroit to the organized-crime families of Chicago, from the dirty South to the gang-infested neighborhoods of L.A. and New York, we all wear the mask. It is the one that says, "I am fearless, I don't care, and I will destroy anything in my path, including myself." But all of us know that beneath this mask is a vulnerable boy whose heart has turned cold.

———

THE NAUSEATING SMELL of spoiled ass, funky armpits, and crusty socks punched me in the nose as soon as I stepped into the cramped bullpen at Wayne County Jail, where intake processing was underway. The stench made my eyes water, and the antiquated ventilation system was doing nothing to help. Before me was a hodgepodge of inmates from all walks of life. I saw veterans of lockdown who had grown accustomed to life behind bars. I saw heroin addicts sprawled across the hardwood benches and urine-soaked floors—some curled in a fetal position, others shaking like scared puppies as they fought the pain of withdrawal. And I saw a few young brothers like me, wide-eyed and waiting for whatever would come next.

Every ten minutes or so, deputies would call another three or four guys into a room and make them exchange their street clothes for the vomit-green uniforms of the jail. Meanwhile, I leaned against the wall in the back, listening to the inmates tell stories—stories in which the storyteller always happened to be the hero. To hear these guys talk, no one here was an addict, and no one was a cheat or a failure. They were badass drug lords. They were the ruthless titans of whole cities who didn't have a worry in the world.

There's a reason why so many inmates use storytelling as a coping tool. Being in prison and stripped of your freedom is painful and degrading, and each day is a fight to maintain your sanity. In order to cope, some inmates make up entirely different lives for themselves, saying anything that might help them seem different or one notch above the rest of us poor, wretched souls. Some have perfected the art of bullshit to the point where they could probably convince George W. Bush that he was Black and only made it through college because of affirmative action.

As I listened to the tales going around the room, I would have traded anything to be back in the 'hood, hustling and drinking with my homeboys. But my reverie was soon interrupted by the sound of an officer calling my name. It was my turn to get dressed out in Wayne County's finest.

I stepped into the hallway with a handful of other inmates and followed the deputy to the dress-out room, which smelled like an ass had just exploded. As I entered, I nearly buckled under the stench.

We were all placed in a line and told to strip. The deputies ordered us to hand them our clothes one article at a time, and when we did, they shook each item methodically, searching for contraband.

Once we had stripped naked, we were ordered to raise our hands above our heads, then lift up our nuts, turn around, and spread our ass cheeks. It was then that I understood why the room had such a horrible smell—it must have been subjected to the exposure of thousands of unwashed assholes over the years. (And I'm not just talking about the officers.)

Soon enough, I was handed my county greens and returned the underwear and socks I had been wearing for days. They were the only personal clothing items we were allowed to keep, and putting them back on reminded me of how much of my life I had forfeited. But the chipping away at my humanity had just begun. Like Dante journeying through the inferno, my life would forever be changed by the things I would witness and take part in—the violence of oppressed against oppressor, predator against prey, and the insane against the criminally insane.

The slamming of the steel doors was a signal that the iron monster had once again been fed. My journey began.

3

"Come up off that shit, li'l nigga!" Tiny raged, holding the nickel-plated pistol to my head.

My heart fluttered like the broken wings of a bird. I was terrified. The cold, steel barrel pressing into my temple pressed into my consciousness a colder reality—at fourteen, I was about to die. The odor of the streets poured from Tiny's body, mingling with the sickly sweet smell of Wild Irish Rose wine, and I struggled to breathe as Tone, Tiny's partner-in-crime, wrapped his crusty arm around my neck. Tiny gripped the gun with his right hand, which was bloated with open sores that bulged with pools of festering, greenish-brown pus. He was a heroin addict and a crackhead, a dangerous combination in a stickup man.

On the streets, it was a well-known fact that dope fiends wouldn't hesitate to kill in order to get their next fix. When crack was added to the mixture in the 1980s, it gave birth to the super-predators who roamed inner-city jungles all around the country, filling the newspapers with stories of unspeakable violence.

The fact that I was young enough to be these guys' son didn't matter to them. All they cared about was the small, white rocks concealed in my underwear. Murdering a child would have been all in a day's work if that's what it took for them to feed their addiction.

Only weeks into my short career as a drug dealer, I had made several crucial mistakes. For one, I had let Tiny and Tone convince me to come outside the safety of the crack house. I had been crazy to trust someone who was one of many victims of the most potently addictive drug at the time, and I hadn't paid attention to my gut instinct, which whispered *Danger, Danger, Danger.* Now I was at the mercy of two desperate men, too numb with fear to scream or plead for my life.

When the initial shock passed, I went into survival mode. I retrieved the plastic bag from my underwear and handed it to Tiny. He then reached into one of my pockets and retrieved a small knot of cash, nearly ripping my pocket off in the process. He stuffed the crack and the money into his pocket and gave Tone the signal to let me go.

I knew what would come next. They were going to shoot me and push me down the basement steps. A week later, one of the tenants would find my decomposed body when the smell became too strong to ignore. I could see the headline of the *Detroit News*: 14-YEAR-OLD FOUND DEAD IN CRACK HOUSE ON JEFFERSON AND CHALMERS.

But instead, Tiny led me to the door of the building, prodding me forward with his pistol. "Get your punk ass away from here," he ordered, shoving me out of the door and onto the cracked sidewalk of Chalmers Street.

A flood of emotions overtook me. I was relieved that I hadn't been killed, but my thin teenaged body trembled with fear as I walked to the Coney Island restaurant on the corner of Chalmers and Jefferson. I was disoriented, unclear as to what I should do. I felt like everyone in the restaurant could sense what had just happened to me. I looked from one unfriendly face to the next, hoping that someone would see the fragile child I was. But all they saw was a designer-clad kid trying to act grown before his time. As I look back on that day, I wonder if what I read as angry glares was really the puzzled faces of people wondering why I didn't have my ass in school.

I wanted someone in that restaurant to stand up and rescue me from the streets. I wanted someone to see a lovable, smart little boy who was hurting inside. I wanted to cry out, but I knew I couldn't because I had vowed never to allow anyone to make or see me cry again. Deep down, I was ashamed of my own fear.

I left the restaurant and walked a couple of blocks, stopping at a phone booth on Kercherval. By the time I dialed my boss's pager, I had convinced myself that anger was the only emotion I felt. There was no way I was going to tell Miko I was scared. I couldn't let anyone in our crew know that the prospect of dying in a urine-soaked hallway didn't sit well with my young mind.

Death wasn't something I had bargained for when I decided to sell dope. I had thought about other things: the money I would make, and all of the clothes I could buy with it. I thought about being able to buy a Honda Elite 150 with a state-of-the-art stereo system. I thought about being able to buy happiness, love, and a safe place to lay my head, but I hadn't thought about the other side of the bargain—the possibility that I could die or forfeit my freedom over a thousand-dollar bag of rocks.

Miko returned my call and told me to meet him back at the original spot on Marlborough and Jefferson, the large white house I had come to loathe. When I got there, the front door was ajar and the smell of decay poured out of every crack. The house had always made me uncomfortable, not in the least because the narcotics unit had made a daily routine of parking a couple of houses down. Some days, they were bold enough to pull directly in front of the spot.

The other reason I didn't like the house on Marlborough was that it was unfit for human habitation. The paint was peeling, and the roof sagged as though it was ready to cave in. The bathtub was full of shit, piss, and dirty clothes. The toilet overflowed with wrappers from the nearby Coney Island, and roaches crawled across the floors and walls in droves. The whole scene was depressing, and the thick stench made me nauseous. In many ways, the house on Marlborough reflected the mentality of the people in the streets. Little did I know, this same sickness was soaking into my pores.

I was nervous as I sat on the porch waiting for Miko to arrive. The sound of rustling came from an overgrown grass lot next door, and I jumped up, ready to fight. But when I turned around, I saw that it was only a stray mutt foraging through the garbage for something to eat. As I calmed my nerves, my thoughts turned to the day I left my mother's house and the chain of events that had brought me here.

MY PARENTS' MARRIAGE deteriorated piece by piece, like an arthritic knee. They would separate and get back together, then separate and get back together again, each reunion giving me a glimmer of hope that things would go back to how they used to be. Their marriage had never been perfect, but our house had always been full of family, food, and great music, and I yearned for those days when my parents were together and happy.

The first time my mom and dad separated, they called me and

my three sisters into the kitchen of our nicely kept brick home on Camden Street. I knew something was amiss, but my eleven-year-old mind was not prepared for the devastating news that would come.

When I was growing up, my parents argued like I imagined any other couple did. But they never berated each other, and their fights never turned physical. So when they announced that they were separating, it stunned us into silence.

"You know things haven't been going that good between me and your father," I recall my mother saying, her voice cracking as she spoke. "So we have decided that it's best for us to separate."

I looked at my father for an answer. The corner of his mouth trembled, and his eyes watered as he looked back at me. Then he spoke.

"Even though things aren't working out between me and your mother, I will always be y'all father," he said, fighting back tears.

I didn't understand what they were talking about. Did separation mean that he would be sleeping on the couch like he did sometimes after they argued? Did it mean he would go and spend a couple of nights at his best friend Clark's house, or come to live upstairs with us? Never did I consider the alternative: my father living in a house that wasn't ours.

When he finally explained that he would be moving to a place in Highland Park that coming weekend, all kinds of thoughts began flowing through my young mind—thoughts about my father and all that he meant to our household. I thought about the holidays and how he would organize us kids to put up the Christmas tree. I thought about how he would give us an allowance every other Saturday so that we could go skating at Royal Skateland. I thought about the sound of him pulling into the driveway each night at approximately 11:45 p.m. when he got off of work.

I was scared. It was as though everything that symbolized family stability had been sucked out of the room. My mother explained that my sisters and I would spend the summer, winter break, holi-day vacations, and weekends at my father's, and we would go to school from her house. The words "her house" stuck in my mind, driving home the reality that our house was no longer "ours." And without my father residing with us full-time, her house could never be the warm, loving home we had once shared.

My father called me to join him downstairs in the basement. As I walked down the steps, my thoughts turned to the many ways our home had changed over the years. I remembered watching my father and uncles hang paneling on the walls while my mother and aunts painted each room, the sounds of Parliament Funkadelic blaring throughout the house. Our home was family central, and every one of my aunts, uncles, and cousins had lived with us at some point. But after that day, our family would never be the same again.

We began packing, and my father outlined what my responsi-bilities would be, now that he was leaving. He told me that I would have to cut the grass and wash the car for my mother. He told me that I was responsible for my younger sisters, who were three and eight years old at the time, and that I had to maintain my honor-roll status at school. We packed some of his records into orange and blue milk crates, each album cover conjuring up visions of the house parties that my parents had thrown in our basement. As he rifled through records by the Isley Brothers, the Ohio Players, the O'Jays, and Marvin Gaye, I took in the images of Afros, platform shoes, and scantily clad women. I thought about my uncle John rousing me from my sleep so that I could come and dance to the sounds of seventies funk while my aunts and uncles cheered me on. The taste of Schlitz Malt Liquor came creeping back as I remem-bered how my uncle Chris or uncle Keith would sneak me a li'l sip to make sure I went right back to sleep when the dancing was over.

I looked at my father as he stared absently at one of the albums. I could sense that he was experiencing the same, deep feeling of sadness. When he looked back up, his eyes were red, and the tears began flowing freely. He hugged me tight and sobbed quietly. His beard scratched my face, the smell of his cologne drifting up my nose as his body heaved with the pain of seeing his family torn apart. We both cried, clinging tightly to each other.

Thinking back, those tears might be the best gift my father has ever given me. He showed me that real men cry, especially when they love deeply.

We packed and cried, and packed and cried, until the crying gave way to laughter and joking. When we were done in the basement, he assured me that he would always be there for me no matter what. To this day, he has never let me down.

OVER THE COURSE of the weekend, we moved my father's belongings to his new home on Pasadena Street in Highland Park. It felt like closure, but little did I know that that weekend would mark the beginning of an emotional roller-coaster ride for our family. After being separated for a little over a year, my parents decided to get back together.

When my parents told us they were reuniting, I was overjoyed. I imagined life returning to normal, and at first, it did. But after a few months, I noticed that my father had begun sleeping on the couch, like he had done before the first time he and my mother separated. They would go days without speaking to each other, and the tender kisses and affection that they had once displayed were replaced with empty stares.

My nights became restless. I stayed up late, waiting for my father to come home from work. I would listen intently when he entered the house, sometimes crawling from my bedroom into the hallway to peek down the stairs into our living room. I held my breath, hoping that instead of looking down to see my father asleep on the couch, I would find the couch empty. But night after night, I was disappointed to see him there, curled up in a ball beneath a blanket. I sensed it was only a matter of time before my parents would be breaking the bad news.

One day, I was playing football in the street with friends when my mother stepped onto the porch and called my name. I took a two-step drop-back, hurled the ball into the air, and yelled, "Terry Bradshaw!" I watched in awe as the ball spiraled down into the outstretched hands of my best friend, Steve, who cradled the cracked leather hide to his chest, ignored the stinging in his hands, and hollered "Lynn Swann!" as he slammed the ball to the ground. Like other kids on the playground, Steve and I believed we were destined for NFL greatness, and we would summon the names of the greats in hopes that it would make us play like them.

But now my mother was calling, and I sulked back to my house. How was I supposed to make it to the NFL if my mother kept breaking up my games to make me run errands? Didn't she realize I needed to practice? But a little smile crept across my face as I realized she had seen me throw a perfect spiral.

When I entered the house, my mother was on her way upstairs to my bedroom, and my focus immediately shifted from football to my mother's movements. Something was off—what was it? Maybe I was in trouble for leaving my room in a mess, or maybe the bathroom I shared with my sisters hadn't been cleaned to her liking.

Her voice cascaded down the stairs as she called my name again. This was the melodious tone of voice that she usually reserved for special occasions, like when we had a house full of company, or when I brought home a good report card.

When I reached my room, she was standing with her back to me, looking at the walls where pictures of my sports heroes and dream cars were taped haphazardly. For a brief moment, I thought she was about to tell me to take them down. I couldn't bear the thought of having to remove my posters of Tony Dorsett or the '69 Cutlass 442. But when my mother turned to face me, tears clung to the corners of her eyes. She pulled me close to her, embracing me in a warm hug, and then inhaled deeply before beginning to speak.

"Pumpkin," she said, using the nickname that my aunt Bebe had given me. "I want you to know, I will always love you no matter what happens. As you know, me and your father have been going through some problems, and we have decided that it's best for us to separate again."

I nodded my head to let her know that I understood, but as her words sank in, my heart began to crumble. I couldn't believe my parents were separating again. They'd promised us that they had fixed things. I had noticed signs of trouble, but that didn't make it any less painful.

And the bad news didn't stop there. "You will have to move in with your father this time," she continued. "I can no longer raise you. You are a young man now, and you will be better off living with your father." With that, she turned away from me.

Those words shredded my heart. How could a mother give up her child? What was wrong with me that made her not want to keep me?

In that moment, I began erecting an emotional wall to protect me from my parents and any other intruder. I was done listening to them, done spending time with them, and done with letting them touch or talk to me. I was tired of being hurt and confused by two people I loved more than anything in the world.

MY PARENTS RECONCILED a second time a year later, but by then, a chasm had opened up between me and my mother. While living with my father, I started smoking cigarettes and developed a keen interest in girls. Because he worked all day, I was used to being on my own and doing what I wanted. I was fourteen now—no way was I going back to conforming to my mother's strict rules.

The first weekend I returned home, I stayed out late at a friend's party. The following morning my mother cursed me out. "Don't bring your ass in my house again that late," she yelled. "I'm not your father, and if you don't like my rules, you can pack your shit and leave."

Every chance I got, I defied my mother's authority. It was my way of punishing her for rejecting me. My father tried to rein me in and support her in her efforts to bring me under control, but it was too late. I had developed an "I don't give a fuck" attitude. The way I saw it, if I didn't care about anything, nothing could hurt me.

My mother responded to this behavior by beating me. I remember her calling me into the bathroom one day when I came home from hanging out with my friends. "Why didn't you put up the dishes like I told you?" she asked—and before I could form a full sentence in reply, she slapped me in my face so hard I could hear ringing in my ears. She then made me strip naked and began beating me with a thick leather belt until my legs and back were full of welts. Her eyes were wild with anger as she swung the belt wildly up and down, tearing into my flesh.

On Sundays, when we went to church, my mother told me to pray to Jesus, and he would answer all of my prayers. Sometimes it gave me hope that she would change if I prayed, but she never did.

It wasn't long before I reached my breaking point. At fourteen, I felt I was too old to accept another ass whopping, and having grown physically stronger, I knew that it wouldn't be long before I lost it and returned the favor for one of my mother's physical assaults. She made a habit of reminding me that I could leave if I didn't want to abide by her rules, so one day, I took her up on that offer and left.

Even as I was leaving, I hoped that she would stay up worrying about me like mothers do. I wanted her to go around the neighborhood, searching for me with tears in her eyes. I wanted her to care for my safety and well-being; I wanted her to hurt in the way that I hurt.

But that never happened, so I turned to the streets.

4

"Man, you ain't gonna believe this shit." My bunky turned to me, rolling a cigarette.

"What happened?" I asked, watching his methodical movements.

"This nigga in the bullpen raped a white boy this morning," he said. He had a puzzled expression on his face, as if he was still trying to make sense of what he had seen.

"Who got raped?" Gigolo asked, approaching our cell door.

"Come on, I'll tell y'all what went down," my bunky replied. He exited the cell and led us to the dayroom, where he lit up a cigarette and sat on the table out front. "This morning when we went down to the bullpen to transfer, this nigga named Seven gave this white boy his cereal and donut. We didn't think nothing of it

33

until we seen Seven talking to him in the back of the bullpen," he explained as he took another drag of his cigarette.

"What happened, dog?" a guy named Twin asked as he walked up to the table.

"Nigga got fucked in the butt in the bullpen," someone said. This sent a trickle of nervous laughter around the room.

It was the first time most of us had come face-to-face with one of the most brutal facts of prison life. We sat there in silence as my bunky continued.

"First, Seven asked the white boy how he was going to pay him back for the cereal and donut he had eaten. The white boy told him he thought he had given him the food because he wasn't hungry and couldn't take it with him. He said it half-jokingly, which seemed to give Seven some kind of thrill. He moved in close to the white boy, massaging his dick, and said that he knew how the white boy could repay him."

I could see my bunky getting uncomfortable, but he continued telling us what happened. "A few motherfuckers started making jokes about how nothing in prison was free. But I don't think they realized how serious Seven was until he put the white boy in a chokehold."

My bunky took the last puff of his cigarette, then thumped the butt across the dayroom.

"He choked the white boy until his face turned blue and he passed out. I never thought he would take it further than that," he said with a distant look in his eyes. "But he did. He dropped the white boy on the floor, rolled him onto his stomach, and pulled down his pants.

"He didn't give a fuck that we were all sitting there," my bunky said, shaking his head. "He pulled his pants down and started fucking the guy."

"That's fucked up," Gigolo said.

"Why y'all ain't stop the nigga?" someone asked.

"What the fuck you mean, why we didn't stop him? Nigga, you know the rules to this shit," my bunky responded angrily.

"Yeah, fool, you know the rules to this shit," Gigolo said in my bunky's defense. "Mind your motherfucking business."

"What the deputies do?"

"I think they were as shocked as we were. They couldn't believe he was raping the guy in front of us like there was nothing wrong with it. And the worst part is, the white boy was only going to boot camp."

"That's fucked up," Twin said. "He should sue these slimy motherfuckers for putting him in the bullpen with that crazy nigga in the first place."

I listened for a little while longer before returning to my cell to think. I had only been in the county jail for two weeks, but I had already learned a great deal. I thought about what it would be like to live the rest of my life around men who were capable of raping another human over something as insignificant as a bowl of cereal or a cigarette. I thought about the psychological breaking point that men in prison reach, and I wondered what kind of mental pressure it would take for me to become a savage, capable of the most reprehensible acts of violence and depravity.

In that moment, I made a promise to myself that I would not leave prison worse than I had entered. I had stood by as adult men and women let drugs strip them of dignity and decency, and I understood the serious nature of the crime I had committed. But I also knew there were some things I would never be capable of, and raping another human being was one of them. Becoming a snitch in order to gain privileges or favor from the guards was another.

Sadly, I would soon learn that not everyone can keep a vow once he finds himself behind bars.

———

THE COUNTY JAIL'S pecking order was as clear as it was unforgiving. From the lowest of the inmates to the highest reaches of the prison staff, life in jail was a real-life human experiment in the survival of the fittest.

A few days after being processed in, I was transferred to the cellblock where I would stay until I was sent up north to prison. As I stepped through the sliding glass doors onto 6 NW, a cellblock where they housed violent offenders, the dayroom grew silent. The only sound I could hear was the raggedy drone of a television that sat atop a metal table. Before walking the short distance across the room to my assigned cell, I scanned the room of black and brown faces, looking out for enemies from the streets or familiar faces from the 'hood.

It felt like every pair of eyes in the room was boring into me. Out the corner of my eye, I noticed a bald, dark-skinned inmate talking to a brown-skinned brother with a long scar on his face. They were whispering to each other and pausing every couple of seconds to look up at me.

My street senses kicked in. I knew immediately that if I was going to have a problem here, it would start with them. From the way the other inmates reacted to them, it was clear that these guys were at the top of the food chain, and I could sense that others in the room were waiting to see what they would do.

As soon as I saw them sizing me up, I returned their glares, sending a clear message that I wouldn't hesitate to fight to the death if need be. But I didn't allow my stare to linger. This was one of the many rules of engagement that I had learned on the streets of Detroit, where staring at someone or stepping on his shoe could get you shot or killed. It was important to let people know that you weren't a pushover, but it was equally important to communicate that you weren't a shit starter, either. It was a delicate balance, but it was the difference between life and death.

I entered my assigned cell and tossed my bedroll onto the top bunk. The only thing I wanted more than freedom was sleep and a hot shower. As I looked around the room, I felt a rising sense of panic. The walls felt like they were closing in on me. I couldn't believe that my life had been reduced to a two-man cell with a toilet. I knew then that I had to figure out how to escape as soon as I could.

A dark-skinned, bald inmate approached my door. I had heard enough to know that the guys on the tier would beat your ass for recreation if there was something they didn't like about you, so I clenched my fist and prepared to deliver the first blow if he got within arm's length.

"You smoke?" the inmate asked as he walked past me to the desk in the back of the cell.

"Yeah," I said, a bit confused, until it dawned on me that this was my cellmate. I had noticed that there were two bunks in the room, but it wasn't like we went around wearing name tags that said, "Hey, I'm your bunky."

"You might want to roll one of these up before they lock us down for the night," he said, passing me a pack of Bugler brand hand-rolled cigarettes as though it was the most natural thing in the world.

I took the pack without knowing what to do with it. I had never rolled my own cigarettes; all I had ever smoked were Newports. I looked at the pack and then back at him as he rolled a thick wad of tobacco into the cigarette paper and left the cell. I followed suit, but my rolling skills were unrefined, and my cigarette came out lopsided.

I stepped out on the rock (our term for the cellblock where we lived) and got a light from the automatic lighter attached to the wall. I inhaled deeply and immediately began choking. The pungent smoke felt like it was ripping my throat to shreds. Everyone laughed as they watched me struggle with the cigarette. It was the worst thing I had ever tasted, but the rush of nicotine felt good, and I was grateful for it.

Moments later, a voice came over the PA system telling us that it was time for lockdown. We returned to the cell, and my bunky introduced himself.

"They call me S," he said.

"Jay," I replied with a nod.

"What they got you for?" he asked, leaning back on his bunk.

"Open murder," I said, studying his face to see his reaction.

"Damn, homie, I hope you beat that motherfucker," he said, leaning forward. "They hit me on a murder and sentenced me to natural life. But I'm about to give this time back." His confidence made me believe him.

We talked deep into the night. S had been locked up for over a year, and he gave me some basic rules to follow if I was ever sent to prison. But he said he thought I could beat my case. I didn't know what he was basing his opinion on, but it gave me hope at a time when hope was the one thing keeping me alive.

I washed my face and upper torso in the sink before hopping onto the bunk. As I lay down, my whole life began rushing through my mind in a violent stream of consciousness. My reality didn't feel real. I couldn't believe I was sitting in a cell with a stranger discussing the possibility of me spending the rest of my life in prison. I was supposed to be on my way to college. I was supposed to be following my dream of becoming a doctor—of becoming a healer, not a destroyer.

I thought of my girlfriend, Brenda. We had lived together for half a year, and she was about four months pregnant. I had a daughter from a previous relationship, but the mother hadn't allowed me to be a part of raising that child. When Brenda told me she was pregnant, I was excited at the thought of being a full-time father for the first time in my life.

A deep sadness engulfed me as I thought about the baby growing inside of Brenda's womb and the conversation we had the night before I was arrested. I had looked into her eyes and told her that everything would be all right, that we would get away from Detroit and get a fresh start. We would give our child the life we had dreamed of as children.

She laid her head on my chest and looked up at me with tear-filled eyes. I rubbed her belly, where our precious baby was growing.

"Can you feel it?" she asked as she guided my hand. The warmth of her belly coupled with the warmth I felt in my heart made me believe everything would be all right. I couldn't believe that I wouldn't be around to see our baby born.

I thought about the embarrassment and disappointment that I knew my father felt over my arrest. I hadn't spoken with him, my stepmother, or my mother since that night; I had made a decision to live the street life, and I felt like I had to deal with the consequences on my own. I had no idea what it meant to be a parent. No idea how it felt to hurt because you knew your child was hurting. It wasn't until years later that I would learn about the sleepless, tearful nights that my father endured during the years of my incarceration.

I couldn't stop the flow of thoughts. I thought about how it felt to fire the shot that ended another man's life. I thought of all the people who had betrayed me—the best friend who turned me in, and the people I knew who had made statements against me. As soon as I was arrested, my friends from the outside turned their backs on me. I hadn't been gone a week, and they had already begun stealing my clothes and playing on the little money I had left.

Then I thought about the ultimate betrayal: my betrayal of myself. This was the hardest thought for me to deal with. I had given up on myself when I picked up drugs, alcohol, and guns. In fact, I had never even given myself a chance in the first place. I thought about every teacher and parent who had told me I was wasting my potential and asked me why I was doing it. Hell, even the officers who arrested me asked me why I was wasting my life. The very people who put me in prison believed in me more than I believed in myself.

But none of that mattered here in the county jail, a place that housed the broken dreams of people like me. The only thing that mattered to me was the threat of a life sentence hanging over my head.

As I drifted off to sleep, I could only manage one thought: *It can't end like this.*

OVER THE NEXT few weeks in the county jail, I was given a crash course on how to survive behind bars. I learned to barter for food or cigarettes with services like making three-way phone calls for other guys or writing a letter for someone who couldn't write. I learned that jail wasn't much different from the streets; it was a power-based environment where the only means of gaining respect were violence and money. Every inmate had to prove himself at some point, and if you had money, you had to prove that you could keep it or find someone who could keep it for you.

Once I was settled in, I called Georgia, a lady from the block who I knew could help me connect with my family. She was like a big sister to me, and I could hear concern in her voice as she asked me about life on the inside. It was through Georgia that I talked to my family and the few friends I had left. She would make three-way calls or have the person I wanted to talk to come by her house.

The first day I called, Georgia went and got Brenda for me. I could hear the worry and the childlike vulnerability in Brenda's voice, and a wave of guilt surged through me. I had never thought about the fact that by getting locked up, I was also imprisoning everyone who loved or cared about me.

For the first few minutes, we talked about what was going on in the 'hood. We talked about my defense strategy and what I needed to do to beat the case. We also talked about some money issues that she was facing, and I told her that I would talk to a few people to help her out. When I told her the date of my next court appearance, she started crying.

"My stomach is growing, and the baby is kicking," she said.

"I'll be home before the baby is born," I said, my voice barely registering above a whisper.

"I need you here with me right now!" she wailed. "Why does God take everybody I love away from me?"

"I don't know, baby."

"You betta get your ass home," she said. I could tell from her voice that a smile had formed on her tear-streaked face.

Brenda was a tough girl who had grown up in tougher circumstances, yet she had the most beautiful laugh that I had ever known. At the time of my arrest, we had still been getting to know each other. But as I listened to her on the other end of the phone, I realized that I truly loved and cared about her, and there was no way I could leave her out there to fend for herself and our child. She deserved to be taken care of, and she deserved to have the father of her child by her side.

She deserved for me to get out of jail, and I vowed that I would give her what she deserved—or die trying.

AFTER TALKING WITH Brenda, I was emotionally and mentally drained, and the last thing I wanted to do was talk to anyone on the rock. I was walking back to my cell when Twin commented on the call, which he had overheard.

"That nigga Jay just got off the phone sucker stroking," he said with a laugh.

A few guys laughed at his joke. To openly express your emotions was considered a weakness, so whenever someone showed any feelings toward a female, be it love or anger, they would say he was sucker stroking. Twin was just joking, but I wasn't in the mood.

"Stay out my business, bitch ass nigga," I said, turning toward him. It was time to show that I could handle my business.

"Damn, nigga. I was just bullshitting," he responded. The whole room grew silent.

"You don't know me like that to be playing, so stay the fuck out my business," I continued, my anger growing.

But Twin didn't take the bait. I could tell that he was at a loss for words.

"Come on, homeboy, let that go," an older cat named L said, guiding me toward my cell.

L was from the Cass Corridor, and he was one of the oldest guys on the rock. All of us respected him, and he was the go-to guy whenever we needed advice. He would sit and talk to us about life, the Bible, and prison. His advice was insightful and articulate, and he was genuine in his concern for us. He had been to prison before, and even when he was on the outside, he was a prisoner to a heavy crack addiction. Like many of the guys who find themselves in the penitentiary, L was at his best in an institutional setting, safe from the temptation of drugs.

When we reached my cell, L came inside and asked me what was going on. I gave him the rundown, and we sat around kicking it about life and the time we were facing. After about half an hour, Twin showed up at the door. He apologized for his comments, and I apologized for snapping on him. We were all going through some tough times, each of us coping in the best way we knew.

———

AFTER MY DISPUTE with Twin, guys on the rock started look-ing at me differently. They began to seek me out for advice, and I slowly emerged as a leader. Older inmates sometimes asked for my help with their problems, and they would defer to me when ever a dispute arose. L took this all in and gave me counsel along the way. He later told me that I reminded him of himself at an earlier age. He said that he had always been smart, but could never pull himself away from the allure of the streets and drugs.

Out of all the young guys, I developed the strongest bond with Gigolo, a brother from Inkster. We were a lot alike, except Gigolo liked to fight more than I did, which made a lot of the guys on the rock keep their distance from him.

Every day, Gigolo and I would sit in my cell or Twin's cell and kick it about life and all the things we missed. Sometimes we would take turns peeking out of the spots in the windows where the paint had peeled away. If you looked at the right angle, you could see outside and catch a glimpse of the courthouse steps and hundreds of people walking by. Looking out that window made it feel like we were stealing a small sliver of freedom.

Each day, at approximately one o'clock, Twin's girlfriend would come and stand outside where he could see her, a sign of her love for him. During that time, we allowed Twin to have the window to himself. In fact, it was our respect for Twin's girlfriend that even-tually led to one of the first physical conflicts I experienced in jail.

A tall, slim, brown-skinned brother from the East Side had moved onto our rock. He seemed cool, so we allowed him to play cards and shoot ball with us. Over the course of the next week, he started coming to our little counseling sessions in Twin's cell.

One Saturday morning, we were all sitting around smoking cigarettes and talking about the court dates that some of us had coming up. We had all gone to the law library, but most of the books were torn up or outdated, so we relied heavily on the advice of L (who was familiar with the law from his previous stints in prison) and the advice of our attorneys. After talking about the pros and cons of taking a plea deal, we were getting ready to lock down for the afternoon count when Twin noticed that a picture of his girlfriend was missing. Gigolo, L, and I hadn't seen it, so we began helping Twin look for the picture.

It was then we realized that the new guy was gone. I shot out of Twin's cell and raced down to where he was staying. When I got there, his door was closed, and a towel was hanging on the window, to keep people from being able to see inside.

I told him to open the door. "Hold on," he yelled back. By this time, Twin, Gigolo, and L had come down to the cell. We demanded that the guy open his door, but he told us he was using the bathroom. By now, the rest of the guys on the rock had come to see what all the commotion was about.

I told Gigolo to grab the sheet from his bed and pop the cell door open. We jimmied the lock, and by the time we got in, the guy was flushing the toilet. But even from the edge of the cell, we could see remnants of the picture floating in the water, and in one of the shreds, Twin recognized the dress his girlfriend had been wearing in the photo.

Before the guy could force out an explanation, I punched him in the jaw. I was angry he had violated our trust, and it was time to make him pay. He staggered against the door and tried to cover up as I delivered another punch, knocking him out into the dayroom. Before he could hit the ground, Gigolo and Twin started punching him in the head and face. The guy scrambled to his feet, rushed toward the cellblock door, and started beating on the glass, begging a deputy to rescue him.

His face was bloody and swollen, and L told us to let him be until the deputies came and got him. A deputy we called Tyson came to get the guy. He was one of the few officers who understood and respected us. He knew we had one of the more laid-back rocks and didn't start shit unless we had a good reason.

When Tyson asked the guy what happened, we looked at one another and started laughing. Twin explained to the deputy that the guy had tried to jack off to the picture, and Tyson began laughing along with us. He turned to the guy and said, "I should send you back in there so they can beat your ass again."

IN A COUNTY jail known for being a hellhole, we had managed to carve out a decent life for ourselves. But the following week, things took a somber turn as we were reminded of the reason all of us were there in the first place. A laid-back guy named G was the first inmate on our rock to be found guilty on the charges he was facing. He was convicted of posing as a police officer and robbing a couple of drug dealers, who had come to court and testified against him. The night before G went for sentencing, we had stayed up talking about the possibilities and what he hoped for. He knew the charge carried a life sentence, but he thought the judge would give him no more than ten years.

When he returned from sentencing and told us he had been given eighty-five years, we were stunned into silence. Each of us started thinking about the time we were facing. If they had given G eighty-five years for robbery, what would they give me for murder?

Later that night, I was in my cell kicking it with Gigolo and L when G came to the door to tell me he needed to speak with me. Gigolo and L got up and left so the two of us could talk in private. I could tell by the look on G's face that something was troubling him.

After he pulled the door closed, he lifted up his shirt to reveal a steel pipe concealed in his waistband. "I know how we can get out of here," he said.

5

East Side Detroit

1986

I had been out in the hot sun on Newport Street for nearly an hour, trying to hustle up on a few dollars, but I wasn't having any luck. Each time the wind blew, the stench from my body made my eyes burn. I felt ashamed of my dusty red Levi's and grungy, days-old T-shirt. My hair was dirty from sleeping on the floor of my friend Ernie's basement, and I couldn't remember the last time I had showered or brushed my teeth.

It had been two weeks since I left home.

I watched a short, light-skinned woman leaving the grocery store on the corner of Harper and Newport. Her shopping cart was full of bags, and I wondered if I could convince her to give me something to eat. The only thing I had eaten that day was a piece of buttered toast that Ernie had smuggled me in the morning. By now, my stomach had passed the stage of growling and was barking like a full-grown dog.

When the woman stepped onto the parking lot, I approached her swiftly while her back was turned. She saw me out of the corner of her eye, but before she could protest, I retrieved two of the bags from her grocery cart.

"Allow me to help with these, ma'am," I said, mustering as much charm as I could.

She turned around, clutching her purse and looking like she was ready to scream. I revealed my yellow, gap-toothed smile and proceeded with the bags to her car, where I waited for her to open the trunk. After a long moment, she relaxed and popped the back hatch, and I began loading each bag into the trunk.

When I was done, she reached into her purse and took her wallet out. "I don't have much," she said, pulling two shiny quarters from her purse.

I took them and stuffed them in my pocket, prepared to walk away. But she called me back.

"Here, take this and get you something to eat," she said. She reached into her purse and pulled out a food stamp that was worth a dollar.

I took it with a smile and rushed inside the grocery store. I grabbed a grape Faygo soda, a bag of Better Made Hot! Chips, and a pack of cookies. When I came out of the store, I checked to make sure the coast was clear, then darted into the alley behind the grocery store. I kneeled down beside the dumpster and ripped open the bag of chips. The stench of rotted food coming from the dumpster wasn't enough to spoil my appetite, nor were the maggots that were feasting on a pool of reddish liquid next to me. I greedily stuffed handfuls of chips into my mouth and chased each round with a gulp of the sweet, purple soda. I was so hungry, it felt like my stomach would start eating my spine if I didn't get the food down fast enough.

Once my stomach started filling up, I stood and exited the alley. I knew Ernie would enjoy some of the cookies and the rest of the chips I had in the bag, but I had wanted to make sure I was full before I shared my rations.

My Fila tennis shoes were on their last leg as I walked down Newport toward Wade. I had to walk with my toe curled to keep it from dragging on the ground through the hole in the bottom of my shoe. As I walked past each street, nearing the one where my parents lived, my palms started sweating.

The last thing I wanted was for my mother to see me in this condition. So far, she had been right—moving out was a bad idea. I hadn't thought through my exit strategy, and by the time I realized it was extremely hard for a child to make it in an adult world, my pride and stubbornness wouldn't allow me to go back. I didn't want to hear her say, "I told you so," and I didn't want to return to a place where I felt unwanted.

I breathed a sigh of relief when I reached Camden and didn't see anyone I knew. It was still early, so there weren't many people out on the block. I looked down toward my mother's house and saw her Monte Carlo sitting in the driveway. A twinge of sadness shot through my body as I thought about how my life used to be. But I stuffed that feeling back down and kept walking until I reached Wade.

Before I made it to the corner, I could see everyone was out at the house next door to Ernie's. I groaned inside when I noticed a few of the older guys from my neighborhood hanging out on the porch. It was a 'hood custom for us to crack jokes on one another on the street, and nothing was off-limits. The more uncomfortable the target became, the more the crowd laughed. For the last week or so, I had been on the butt end of jokes about my clothes and hygiene, but the most painful part came at the end of the day, when the older guys cracked jokes about me not having anywhere to go. I felt like a bum. I tried to laugh along with them, thinking it would prove that their words didn't faze me—but underneath, I was being torn to shreds. There were even moments when I got so angry that I wanted to fight, but that made everyone laugh harder because, at only five-foot-six and 110 pounds, I wasn't going to beat any of them.

Ernie came to the door and let me in. I handed him the leftover chips and cookies and went straight down into the basement, where a mix tape was playing on Ernie's boom box. A few minutes later, my friend Tommie Seymour came over, and we talked about our plans for the day. Tommie and Ernie were the only ones who seemed to understand what I was going through at home, and they had done everything they could to help me out.

By the time we stepped back outside, most of the guys next door were gone, so we went and sat on Kurt's porch. After a few moments of sitting and talking, we heard the sound of deep bass coming from down the block. We looked around, waiting to see who would come driving by with their music thumping. It was the newest phenomenon erupting in 'hoods all across the city.

Our neighborhood was home to some of the most notorious drug gangs of the crack era. From the Best Friends and the Chambers Brothers to White Boy Rick (who grew up around the corner from us), our streets were flooded with these new neighborhood superstars. The sounds blaring from their fancy rides drew attention and envy from all the younger guys and girls in the 'hood. They would zip past in their Jeep Wranglers or Jeep Cherokees, the music thundering out of the back, and we would all stand around talking to one another about our dream rides. For the first time in our young lives, we saw guys our age living the American Dream, and we all wanted a share of it.

Moments after we heard the sound of the music, a small, white Dodge Omni stopped at the corner.

"That's Miko," Tommie said. He left the porch and walked

over to greet the tall, muscular, light-skinned man in the driver's seat. We watched from the porch as the two of them talked. After a minute, Tommie came back and told us what they had discussed. He said Miko was looking for someone to "roll" for him, which was code for selling drugs. He said Miko was paying up to $350 a week, plus $10 a day for food, for anyone willing to sit in one of his drug spots. The only catch was that you had to be willing to sit in the spot twenty-four hours a day, seven days a week.

Ernie didn't want to do it, and Tommie said he couldn't. They both turned to me, and I already knew what they were thinking: rolling for Miko would be a way for me to get off of the streets. It was the lowest job on the drug-dealing totem pole, but it sounded like a good deal to me. All I could think about was having somewhere to lay my head and a way to feed and clothe myself. Without further discussion, I told Tommie that I would do it.

Tommie walked back to the car and told Miko I was down to roll. Miko called me over, and when I got there, he asked me my name. I told him that my name was Pumpkin, the nickname my aunt had given me as a kid.

"You got to come up with another name, li'l homie," Miko said, taking in my unwashed appearance. "What's your real name?" he asked.

"James," I responded as I thought about a new nickname.

"You should call yourself Jay," he suggested.

"Yeah, that sound slick," I said, rolling my new nickname around in my head.

After talking with Tommie for a few more minutes, Miko told me to hop in the passenger seat, and we sped off with the sounds of Cybotron beating from the speakers. It was the perfect soundtrack for our neighborhood, with the fast-paced beat of techno-house music matching the frantic rhythm of our young lives.

"You had something to eat yet?" Miko asked.

"Some chips and cookies," I replied.

"I'ma shoot up to Burger King before we go over to the spot."

"All right," I said as houses and cars zipped by on the other side of the window.

We reached the Burger King on Gratiot, which was a stone's throw from the Ninth Precinct of the Detroit Police Department. Miko turned down the music as we pulled into the parking lot. When we got out of the car, a police cruiser pulled out of the lot, and I felt a nervous energy course through my body. I wasn't thinking about what would happen if I were caught selling drugs, nor did I think about the fact that I could get killed or charged with any number of crimes that were associated with the business. All I knew was that it felt exciting to be rolling with a badass like Miko.

We grabbed some food and headed over to a street named Flanders, where Miko's spot was located. The house was a dilapidated duplex that sat in the middle of the block, and it looked like it would fall over if the wind blew too hard. The splintered porch steps creaked as we ascended them, and a dark-skinned, slender woman greeted us when we reached the porch.

"Hey, Miko," she said, opening the door for us to come inside.

"What's up, Dee," Miko replied. We stepped into the darkened living room.

The woman gave me a once-over and turned back to Miko. "Who's the li'l man?" she asked.

"This my little brother, Jay," he said, introducing me. "He gonna be holding down the spot over here."

He retrieved a plastic bag from his underwear and walked toward the dining room table. "Where that mirror at?"

"I got it," Dee said as she followed him into the room.

Miko held up the bag for me to see. "These are nickels," he explained. "It's a hundred rocks in this bag, and they go for five dollars apiece."

"All right," I said, nodding my head.

"How much does that come up to?" he asked.

"Five hundred dollars," I said.

"Okay, li'l nigga. I see you can count. All the sacks I give you will be the same," he said, "but it's up to you to count them. That way, you'll know I ain't cheating you."

Miko was teaching me an important rule of the game. In the world of dealing crack, no one is to be trusted. It is a predatory and parasitic environment, and nearly everyone is out to get over in some way, even if it meant cheating their friends and employees.

Dee returned with a mirror, and Miko poured out the contents of the bag, counting the rocks into piles of twenty. I watched his every move and did the math in my head. I was amazed that such a tiny bag could hold a small fortune.

"When you sell the first two rocks, keep that for your food and cigarettes or whatever you want for the day. When you get down to the last twenty rocks, call me so I can bring you some more, all right?"

"Yeah," I said, and I took the bag from him.

"Keep the sack in your drawers, and don't let anyone else hold it. When someone comes through, Dee will let you know if they are straight. Don't show them shit until they show you the money. And don't sit there and haggle with them over the size of the rock. This ain't the store, and the customers aren't always right. But at the same time, treat them the way you want to be treated."

"I got you," I responded. I was playing cool, but on the inside, the excitement of my new world was taking over.

"Let me show you where the heat at, in case somebody get out of line," he said. He led me into the back room and pulled a sawed-off shotgun from beneath a soiled mattress.

I had never held a shotgun before, and I was intimidated by the menacing look of it. It looked like it would knock me to the ground if I pulled the trigger, but when Miko handed it to me, I took it and held it like I knew what I was doing.

"That button right there is the safety," he said. "If a nigga get out of line, take the safety off, point it at him, and shoot. Trust me, this will tear they motherfucking head off."

I didn't know what to say. Somehow I hadn't thought about the possibility of having to shoot anyone. I didn't know yet that crack could turn people into stone-cold killers. I had seen people smoking weed and drinking, but the most that ever happened was a fistfight.

"I'm going to pick up your partner, Tee," Miko said. "He good people, and he'll have your back, but this is your spot. So run it the way you want it run."

With that, he turned the spot on Flanders over to me. I was off the streets and open for business.

TEN MINUTES AFTER Miko left, my first customer showed up. Dee met him at the door and told me what he wanted. I came to the door, and he handed me a crumpled twenty-dollar bill through the bars of the Armor Guard. In return, I gave him four rocks. He looked them over and smiled before leaving the porch.

It was my first sale. As I looked at the money in my hand, it all started to feel so real. I was officially a drug dealer.

Within a few hours, customers were streaming through the door like water. My pockets were quickly filling up with five-dollar bills, until I had a fat knot bulging from my pants pocket.

The first week flew by, and I was excited when Miko came through to pay me. He deducted $75 for the rocks I had traded for clothes that some of the customers were selling. I felt rich holding the $275 dollars he had given me in small bills. That wad was the most money I had ever had. He told me to call when I was finished, and he would take me out to Eastland Mall to shop.

When we hit the mall later that day, I couldn't wait to go to Foot Locker and cop a crispy pair of Filas, which at the time were the hottest shoes you could get. I felt like a king when I pulled out my knot of money and paid for the shoes. It was the first time I had been able to walk into a store and buy exactly what I wanted without having to worry about how much it cost. We continued shopping, and Miko bought me some other items to go with my gear. He seemed to be embracing me like a little brother, and he told me he always wanted me to look fresh.

I felt like a superstar the next time I walked down my block. At the age of fourteen, my wardrobe cost more than those of the adults in my 'hood. Like most teenagers, I wanted to be accepted and exalted by my peers, and when I came through wearing my fresh Filas, Ballys, and Jordans, I could hear the girls talking about how good I looked. The attention was every bit as addictive as the drugs that I was selling.

Within a few weeks, I had immersed myself fully in my new life as a hustler. The money came quick, but I found ways to spend it quicker. I decked myself in the latest gear, and I felt proud, walking around with a wad of money in my pocket. But in truth, I was over-compensating for the things that had been missing in my life—the most important of which were love and acceptance, things my new life couldn't give me. I wouldn't admit it to myself at the time, but I felt lonely. Tee was a few years older, so there wasn't much we had in common besides making fast money, and I couldn't relate to Dee or her husband because they were high all of the time. They never smoked crack in front of me, but I could tell when they were high because they would start acting jittery and paranoid.

One day, a customer named John came through to buy some rocks. John was what we called a "runner," someone who would make a run to the crack house for a gathering of smokers who hung out at his house. They would give him their money, and he would find the best spot to get them what they wanted. John was a frequent customer, usually buying two or three hundred dollars' worth of rocks at a time. But this time, after buying a hundred and fifty dollars' worth of rocks, he asked if we would be interested in rolling out of his house. He told me he had a spot on Wilshire that he was interested in opening, and I told him that I would run it by Miko.

I called Miko to tell him about John's offer, and he told me we could check it out. When he came to pick me up, Miko said he was proud of me for thinking of ways to expand the business. If things went right, he promised he would take care of me.

John lived three houses off of the corner of Wilshire and Chalmers. The street was lined with well-kept brick Colonials and Tudors, and John lived in a big, pretty brick house that was a stark contrast to our house on Flanders. Miko asked me if I was sure I had the right house, and I double-checked the address that John had written down and told Miko we were in the right spot.

John came to the door and invited us inside. We were surprised to find that his house still had the appearance of a normal home and not a crack house. There were relics of John's former life as a middle-class family man. Framed pictures of his wife and children were hung on a wall in the dining room, and the living room was well furnished with a floor-model television and sectional couch. I half expected the woman of the house to descend from the stairs and ask if we wanted refreshments, but instead, we got down to business.

John told us the story of how he lost his job, his wife, and his kids as a result of smoking crack. He was in a desperate spot, and allowing us to sell out of his house would allow him to keep his home and support his habit. It was a good deal for us, so we took him up on it and moved in the next week.

———

DURING THE EMBRYONIC stages of the crack epidemic, my old neighborhood was still one of the nicer neighborhoods on the East Side of Detroit. Most of the houses maintained pristine exteriors, but on the interior, the families were being slowly consumed by the madness of addiction. The promise of the Black middle class was eroding as crack and all of its associated vices entrenched themselves deep into the heart of the 'hood. In the sixties and seventies, it was heroin that had wreaked the havoc, but the damage caused by crack would make heroin seem like little more than a footnote.

We set up shop in John's house on Wilshire and quickly developed what would become the go-to business model for inner-city hustlers. We installed an Armor Guard door between the kitchen and the stairway leading to the basement, so that our customers could walk right in instead of clustering around the front door while they waited to be served. If a customer wanted to stay and smoke, John would charge them a couple of dollars or a piece of their rock. It worked to our benefit because some of the customers would end up staying down there all day, smoking up their entire paycheck in the basement.

John had a lot of friends who smoked, and most of them had steady incomes from jobs at the many factories throughout the area. Our spot was one of the first in that part of the neighborhood, a convenient spot for upscale clients like them. The only competition we had came from some guys who had a spot a couple of blocks over, but their rocks were small by comparison, so they didn't pose any threat to us.

After a few days of working upstairs, I grew bored of sitting by myself and decided to venture down into the basement. That was my first time seeing anyone smoke crack. I sat behind the bar with the shotgun and took in the scene, which looked straight out of a movie. There were mirrors, razor blades, and pipes spread across the bar, next to a bottle of 150-proof Old Florida Rum, which the customers would use to make torches. I watched men and women smoke their pipes with such intimacy that it looked like they were making love. A look of ecstasy would come over them when they inhaled the thick, white smoke into their lungs, and I found it mesmerizing. I had never witnessed anything transform a person so quickly or dramatically.

What blew my mind was that the drug seemed to affect each of them in a different way. There were some who got so paranoid that they hid in the closet beneath the stairs or jumped behind the bar and sat curled up in a ball on the floor. The rest smoked and went into a trancelike state.

A week after my first trip to the basement, a lady who lived around the corner stripped all of her clothes off and ran out of the house naked. She said that someone was chasing her. John ran after her and eventually brought her back into the house, where she sat naked at the bar smoking. I tried not to stare at her breasts or the triangle of hair between her legs, but I couldn't help myself. I was intrigued by the female anatomy, a fascination that was only just beginning.

Another day, I was down in the basement serving a customer when I noticed a man crawling across the floor, picking up every white speck he could find. The other customers told me that he was "ghosting," meaning he had smoked all of his crack and was hallucinating that the floor was covered with rocks. This became a common occurrence in the basement. It was crazy, watching grown men and women on their knees, searching the basement floor for a crumb of crack. At the time, I was ignorant about their plight and the seriousness of addiction, so I laughed at them until my stomach felt like it was going to burst. I didn't realize it then, but I was growing desensitized to the suffering of others and developing a warped view of adults and authority.

For our first month on Wilshire, the money flowed in a steady stream. Every personality type imaginable came through the door. Our clientele consisted of white people, Black people, men, women, and people from the suburbs all the way down to the ghetto. Some of the best boosters in Detroit would also come through the house. For just a few rocks, they would sell us leather coats and silk shirts that were worth hundreds of dollars. They sold me televisions, VCRs, and handguns for little to nothing. I wasn't old enough to drive, but I could rent Cadillacs, Monte Carlos, and Regals for a couple of hours, all in exchange for a couple of rocks. These people ran errands for me, lied for me, and would have killed for me—or killed me. All for the love of crack.

Women would come over to clean up the house and wash our clothes for a rock. Things always started off innocent, but it wouldn't be long before they were cleaning up naked. This was during the early days of the epidemic, when crack was still considered a glamorous drug, so the women coming through were still attractive and dressed with pride and dignity. Sex was there for the taking. Women who were married and had children older than me would offer to give blowjobs or fuck the entire crew in exchange for rocks. Within a few months, these same women would develop the visible signs of addiction—dirty clothes, bloodshot eyes, and muddled hair.

I was working one of our spots one day when a customer whom everyone called the "Head Doctor" came through. She was so proficient with her oral skills that she would offer you a money-back guarantee—and that day, she set her sights on me. There I was, fourteen years old, standing against the side of a crack house and getting a blowjob, an experience I had thought was reserved for grown men.

Like many women who came through the spot, the Head Doctor said all the right things, making me feel and think that it was okay to be having sex with a grown woman. I went along with it, unaware that beneath the excitement, she was a drug-addled pedophile who preyed on the raging hormones of young drug dealers.

Nevertheless, it felt empowering to be fourteen years old and have sexual command over grown women. They made me feel like my pleasure was the only thing that mattered, and before long, I couldn't relate to girls my age anymore—they weren't ready to do the things I was accustomed to doing. I had been raised to respect and honor women, but in this new world, those rules no longer applied. Looking back, I believe the crack epidemic is partly to blame for the misogyny in our community, and in hip-hop culture. When I was growing up, it was nearly unheard of for men to refer to women as hoes and bitches, but in the streets, these terms became the norm.

Day by day, we were all being stripped of our morals. It was hard to respect people who didn't respect themselves, and disrespect grew in proportion to the deceit and manipulation that we experienced dealing with our customers. We learned through trial and error that no one was to be trusted.

The most important lesson I learned was that crack was nothing to be played with. It wreaked havoc in people's lives and destroyed families. I witnessed people I had admired growing up fall prey to the pipe. Guys I once looked up to were now groveling at my feet, begging for rocks on credit. I saw women who were at one time beautiful teachers, homemakers, students, or store clerks reduced to strung-out crack whores.

Over the summer, Miko opened up a few more spots throughout our neighborhood. We operated like any other corporate structure, expanding into other areas at will and taking advantage of new clientele. At the time, I was making ten dollars off of every hundred dollars' worth of rocks that I sold, plus an extra two dollars in tops—the street hustler's built-in gratuity. Instead of selling five-dollar rocks, we were now selling bigger ones for twelve dollars. I went from making $350 a week to making $300 in profit from every thousand-dollar sack that I sold. On a good day, we could move three to four thousand dollars' worth of rocks.

Miko was making a lot of money off of my hustling and dedication, but as I sat in his spots twenty-four hours a day, I never would have guessed that I was being exploited. All I knew was that I stayed fresh and my pockets were fat. I didn't have long-term plans or an exit strategy. All I cared about were the shoes and clothes I wore and the things other people thought about me.

I was losing my focus, my respect for the community, and ultimately, my own identity. I began morphing into a callous, apathetic, coldhearted predator. Compared to the guys I ran with, I wasn't as quick to get angry or resort to violence. But anger and violence were a necessary part of the dope game, and it wouldn't be long before I would have to employ them if I wanted to survive.

6

I stood at the front door of our small ranch home on Blackstone Street, the familiar surroundings filling me with anticipation as I waited for Brenda to answer the door. My heart raced as I listened to her steps approaching from inside.

Brenda opened the door with an angelic smile on her face, and rushed into my arms.

"I missed you so much," she said, holding me tight and covering my face with feather-soft kisses.

"I told you I was coming home one way or another," I said, wrapping my arms around her in a tight embrace.

———

SOMEONE TAPPED ON my cell door, and I woke up. Normally I would have been pissed if someone woke me from a dream like that, but this time, I was smiling. I knew I was about to turn my dream into reality, and it would only be a matter of time before I saw Brenda again.

It was two o'clock in the morning, and I knew that the shadowy figure standing on the other side of the door was likely to be Gigolo. He and I had developed a method for getting out of our cells whenever we felt like it, to smoke and use the phones. We would tie a knot in a sheet, slide the knot into the doorjamb, and shake it until the latch popped open. The deputies were never in the control center on our wing, and we had studied their rounds to the point where we knew when they were coming and going.

"I need to holla at you for a minute," G said, sliding the knotted sheet beneath my door. We popped the door open, and I grabbed a couple of squares before walking with G to the dayroom.

"Wassup?" I asked as I fired up the square.

"I think Gigolo and Jabo want to roll with us," he said.

"You talked to them?"

"Yeah, but I didn't go into detail about what we were going to do."

I was relieved that he hadn't said anything about our plan, because I wanted to be present at all discussions regarding the escape. Even though G had sparked the idea, I became responsible for planning and execution when he recognized that his plan—bludgeoning an officer and taking his uniform—would never work. My plan, however, was foolproof!

"Let's see if they're woke," I whispered, putting out my cigarette.

We crept over to Gigolo's cell. When I peeked in, I could see him sitting at the desk, talking to his bunky. I tapped the window and he came to the door.

"Let me holla at you for a minute," I said.

We popped the door, then went and got Jabo. I asked them what they thought about trying to escape from the county jail. Jabo hadn't been to court yet, but knew he was facing a lot of time, and Gigolo was still waiting to go to trial. My sentencing date was only weeks away, so I felt like I had nothing to lose. But their situations were different, and I wanted to be sure that they would be down to rock with us before I told them what was up.

They said they were down to bust out as soon as we could put the plan in motion. I told them we would leave that Sunday, which gave us five days to plan.

I wanted to tell L about our escape, but I knew he would try to talk me out of it. L was a Christian, a real religious brother who often quoted from the Bible. We respected his wisdom, but at the time, I wasn't willing to trust my freedom to a God I couldn't see. For the four years I was on the streets, the only thing I believed in was the power of money and guns, so I wasn't about to allow L to talk me out of our plan, nor did I want to hear a sermon about trusting the Lord. I wanted to be free so that I could be with Brenda and our unborn child.

Gigolo suggested we get as many sheets as we could from the guys on the rock and the deputy who passed them out. I hid the pipe in my mattress and we waited patiently for Sunday night to roll around. We did our best to conceal our excitement from the rest of the guys on the rock, but when we were alone in one of the cells kicking it, we couldn't stop talking about what we would do when we got out. We talked about the food we would eat, the sex we would have, the alcohol we would consume, and the piles of money we would make.

During that week, I talked to Brenda nearly every day. She gave me updates on the growth of the baby in her womb, and we talked about all the things we missed about being together. We continued to plan a life together despite the fact that I was waiting to be sentenced. I kept telling her that I would be home soon, but she couldn't have guessed how far I would go to make that promise a reality.

WHEN SUNDAY ROLLED around, we spent the day making our final preparations. We gathered the food we had collected from the commissary and made sure everyone had extra socks and a T-shirt to change into when we made it down to the streets. In the county jail, we weren't allowed to have gym shoes, so we decided the best thing to do was pull a few pair of socks over our shower shoes to absorb the blow when we hit the ground.

All day, it felt like time was moving in slow motion, until finally the night arrived. After the deputy completed his 2 a.m. rounds, Gigolo popped his cell door and came down to my cell. He had his county shirt tied around his face like a ninja. I wrapped my face the same way and helped him pop my cell door. My bunky asked what was up, and I told him to go back to sleep. He and I never really spoke, so he went with the program. I had slid the pipe out of my mattress before lockdown that night, and I grabbed it now as I prepared to exit the cell. It was the first time Gigolo had a chance to hold it.

"Damn, homie, this a bad motherfucker," he said, feeling the weight of the pipe as I helped G pop his cell door.

We went to get Jabo out of his cell, and with the four of us gathered, it was showtime. G was the biggest and strongest among us, so he was the first one to take a turn at breaking the thick Plexiglas window. The first blow sounded like a gunshot. My heart pounded in rhythm with G's strikes to the window, one ferocious blast after another. My body was on fire with adrenaline.

After a minute, G stopped and handed me the pipe. It was hot to the touch. Someone was screaming from one of the cells for us to stop before we got everyone in trouble, but Gigolo went to the guy's window and told him to shut the fuck up and go back to bed. I laughed a little before going to work on the window, beating it senselessly and adding to the damage that G had started.

Finally, the edge of the window gave way and we were able to push it open. I tried to squeeze between the two beams that were inside the frame, but I could only get part of my shoulder through it, so we went to work bending one of the beams. We wedged the pipe between the wall and the beam and rocked it back and forth.

After a few minutes, we had made enough progress to know that we were only minutes away from being able to climb down the tied-together sheets toward freedom. We didn't give a damn that the guys on the rock were hollering at us to go back to our cells. The only thing that mattered to us was getting out.

We kept at it for about ten minutes before we stopped and took turns seeing if we could fit through the window. When we got around to me, I tried to fit my head through the beams. Just as I was working my way through to the fresh air outside, a female voice hollered up to the window from the street.

"Hey, what are you doing?"

I jumped back from the window and told G we had been spotted. One eyewitness could ruin our whole plan, but we decided we had come too far to turn back now, so we went back to work bending the beam. What we didn't realize was that the woman outside was a deputy doing a perimeter check. Within two minutes, a squad car had pulled up and was flashing a light at the window.

"Damn, this is fucked up," I said, turning toward the rest of the crew. My heart sank at the realization that our chances of escape had been ruined.

We looked around at one another, then agreed to go back to our cells. But just as I was walking through my cell door, I realized that we had left the pipe—the most incriminating piece of evidence—in the dayroom. I ran back, grabbed the pipe, and threw it out of the window before rushing back to my cell. I knew the deputies would be rushing the rock any minute now, so I did everything I could to remove any evidence that I had been gone. I removed the socks from my shower shoes, shook the glass out, took off my extra T-shirt, and jumped onto my bunk, pulling the scratchy, wool blanket over my head and doing my best to play sleep.

It took the deputies at least twenty minutes to figure out which rock the escape attempt had occurred on. It felt like the longest twenty minutes of my life. I could hear my heart beating, and I was sure that the deputies would hear it echoing through the dayroom when they opened the door. Finally, a bright light washed over the room as they burst in and turned on all of the lights.

A sergeant barked out orders as the deputies went from cell to cell, snatching each of us out. They slammed us up against the wall and forced us to strip naked in the middle of the dayroom. They threatened to beat our asses and bust our heads with flashlights if we didn't come clean. I imagined that when I turned around, there would be several men standing with their fingers pointing at G, Gigolo, Jabo, and me. But when I turned around, I realized how well we had concealed our identities. Everyone looked confused. No one knew who or how many of us had tried to escape.

The fact that no one said anything seemed to infuriate the deputies, so they tore through our cells like human tornadoes. They threw our pictures, letters, and commissary onto the dayroom floor along with our mattresses. Lucky for our crew, this meant that every inmate present now had glass particles on his property. The crime scene had been contaminated, and when one of the captains realized their error, he ordered us back into our cells.

They told us that we would be on lockdown until they got to the bottom of what happened, and it was this threat that led to someone ratting us out. We never found out for sure who it was, but there was a fifth inmate who had originally planned to go with us, before deciding to back out at the last minute. He was the only other guy who knew of our plot, and we all suspected that he was the one who gave us up.

I lay back on the bunk and fought back tears of defeat. It was five o'clock in the morning. I had never wanted anything so bad in my life, and now the gravity of my situation hit me. I thought about Brenda having to go it alone with our child, and my heart sank. Up to that point, I hadn't made any preparation for being locked away from my family and friends. I also hadn't stopped for one minute to think about the victim of my crime or his family. I was wrapped up in a delusional state of selfishness and denial.

AFTER A FEW hours, the deputies returned to our rock and headed straight for Gigolo's cell. They cuffed him and his bunky and escorted them away. I stood at my window, straining to hear what was going on. Initially, I thought they were doing something routine since they had also cuffed his bunky, but moments later, they came to my cell and told me to step out. They cuffed me, boxed up the rest of my belongings, and told me that I was being placed in the hole and charged with attempted escape.

In the hole, there were no large metal doors and no bunkies— just you alone in your cell with those ominous steel bars looking back at you. The days there crawled by. I spent most of the time lying on the floor, peering through the cracked window at a street where cars drove by all day with their music bumping. If I wasn't doing that, I would watch the roaches crawl down the tier as the other inmates talked through the bars about different aspects of life. Sometimes we would sit back in our individual cells and recite the verses of rap songs that we loved.

Other times, we would kick it about our childhoods. It was through these stories that I learned about the years of abuse and neglect that we all had suffered. We were wounded boys, all of us, and our emotional scars ran deep. Most of us came from homes where ass whoppings were the norm and vile words were tossed out like candy to trick-or-treaters on Halloween. We weren't bad people, but we had made some very bad decisions that were shaped by the bad things we had experienced. We were fathers, brothers, uncles, drug dealers, robbers, and killers. And we weren't any one of those things by itself—what we were was a mixture of failure, neglect, promise, and purpose.

One week later, I was returned to court and sentenced to seventeen to forty years in prison.

7

WILSHIRE STREET
East Side Detroit, Michigan
1986

"The police are outside!" John warned. A loud banging started on the front door, and I rushed downstairs to see what was going on. John was known for being paranoid, but when I looked out of the front window, I saw two squad cars parked out front. I snapped into action. I had less than a minute to get rid of our stash before the cops kicked in the door.

I raced around the house, gathering all of the rocks and throwing them down the heat vent in the dining room. I wasn't sure where they would end up, but I knew for certain that the police wouldn't get them. Once the house was clean, John opened the door, and eight officers rushed in with guns raised. They didn't have a search warrant, and I can't recall whether they asked John for permission to enter. The officers told John that one of the neighbors had witnessed a shooting in the backyard, and they had come to investigate. No one had been shot or killed there that night, and John told the officers as much. But that didn't stop them from rummaging through the house.

From the way our house was set up, it was clear that we were running a drug operation: the Armor Guard; the living room table strewn with leftover Coney Island and bottles of warm Olde English "800" Malt Liquor; piles of unwashed clothes in the corner next to a row of gym shoes. And then there was the basement full of dazed customers, clueless about what was going on.

A middle-aged Black officer and a young white officer ushered me, John, and an older homie, named Lee, into the dining room, as other officers went outside and entered the basement through the side door. I was calm at first because I knew I had gotten rid of all the dope; but then I heard a burst of commotion from downstairs, followed by piercing screams as the police went to work beating our customers. My hands began to shake. The addicts downstairs were screaming like they were on the edge of death, and I had no desire to experience whatever was happening to them.

We were ordered to place our hands on the wall, and the young white officer searched the living room and dining room before turning his attention to us. He patted Lee down and took all of the money he had in his pocket. Lee protested, showing him his check stub, and the officer returned Lee's money. He then came over to me and patted me down, asking where the dope was stashed. He searched my pockets, then stuck his hand in my waistband and pulled it away from my body so that he could see if I had anything stashed in my underwear.

Then, without provocation, he punched me in my nuts. It felt like someone had sucked all of the air out of my body. I grabbed myself and slumped to the floor, where I lay still while he pulled my money from my pocket.

"Tell me where the dope at!" the Black officer said with a smirk on his face as they counted the money they had taken out of my pockets.

I was in too much pain to respond, and if I said what I wanted to say, it would cost me another beatdown. In that moment, I lost what little respect I had for the police. It didn't matter that what I was doing was right or wrong—they had no right to beat a fourteen-year-old kid like that.

Switching tactics, the officers asked me where I had gotten my money. I told them it had come from my uncle. They told me that I was lying, then snatched me up from the floor and slammed my face into the wall. I braced my skinny body for the barrage of blows that I knew was coming, but instead of beating me more, they placed me in handcuffs and told me they were taking me in for loitering in a suspected drug house.

The department never brought charges related to that search, but they turned the confiscated money into evidence. I didn't know the law at the time, but I knew enough about life to know that we would never see the officers or the money again. It was one of the many lessons I've learned over the years about the officers who police the 'hood. I'm not saying that all officers are crooked, but too many of the men and women in blue were no different from us. They were opportunists, and when they saw a chance to get over, they took it.

EVEN AFTER THE raid, the spot on Wilshire was banging. Everyone in the crew was making money. We would ride up to Royal Skateland in Miko's Jeep Wrangler and his Pontiac Grand Am with the music blaring. We would all get out in our Fila suits with our pockets bulging, dancing and talking shit like we owned the 'hood. The girls flocked to us and the guys wanted to be us. I ate it up like it was Thanksgiving dinner.

We were addicted to the life, and as with any other addiction, we were always looking for ways to make it more exciting. Sometimes we would hit Belle Isle, a park on an island in the middle of the Detroit River, and stand around the cars with the music blaring as we sipped on Olde English and smoked weed. But that wasn't enough, and in a matter of months, a few of the guys in our crew had decided to raise the stakes by getting high on fifty-ones— joints laced with crack. I resisted the temptation for a while. I had only just started drinking and smoking weed on a regular basis, and I wasn't trying to take it any further than that.

But one day, Lee came over to the spot on Wilshire to hang out with me and Tee. We knew that Tee was smoking, so we never allowed him to keep the sack, but I didn't know that Lee was also using until I caught him crushing up a rock and mixing it with a small pile of weed in the master bedroom. When he noticed me, he played like it wasn't a big deal. He told me that fifty-ones weren't like smoking from the pipe, because the weed absorbed the effects of the cocaine.

Lee was the epitome of the manipulative older homie—the kind that so many young men in the 'hood grow up admiring. When things aren't going good at home, these guys have all of the answers. When you don't have anywhere to live, they show you how to hustle and take care of yourself. They make you believe that they have your best interests at heart when, in reality, they are the worst kind of predators in our community. Anyone who encourages a child to sell or use drugs is sick in the head, a danger and a threat to those around him. Most of the guys I know serving long prison sentences were introduced to drugs and crime by one of the older guys in the 'hood.

I watched Lee as he lit up the fifty-one. The joint crackled, and I could see the oil from the cocaine burning through the paper.

The thick plume of white smoke smelled sickly sweet, and the effect on Lee was instantaneous. He inhaled again deeply before passing me the joint with a nod. I took it and held it in my hand for a minute before putting it to my lips and drawing on it.

The smoke felt like evil going down into my young lungs. My pulse began beating erratically, and my lips went numb. My whole body felt higher than it had ever felt, and I was sure my heart was going to burst out of my shirt. My conscience began to fuck with me. I got up to look out the window about ten times, checking for the police, and I was certain my mother would appear at the door any minute with a belt in her hand ready to whop my ass.

Lee assured me that what I was feeling was normal. After a while, Tee joined us, and we spent the rest of the night smoking up all of the profit from that sack. I called Miko to get a refill, and while I waited for him, I grew more paranoid. He had warned me to never smoke crack, and I worried that he could tell I was high just from our phone conversation. When he finally showed up, I was really tripping. I thought to myself, *I'm never smoking that shit again in my life.* But I knew even then that I was lying.

BY THE NEXT week, the smoking had become a regular thing. At first, we would pay for it out of our own pockets, but there was no way that our earnings could keep pace with the addictive pull of the laced joints. Between the three of us, we were smoking more than a thousand dollars' worth of rocks a day. My fourteen-year-old world was spinning out of control, faster than I could make sense of it.

Around this time, I was also working a spot on Maiden Street. It was a duplex and we rolled out of the downstairs unit. Kevin, the nephew of the family who lived upstairs, was in his early twenties and used to sell crack himself. We clicked instantly and would stay up all night smoking and kicking it about life. One night, we were up getting high when we decided that, the next time Miko dropped off a thousand-dollar sack, we should run off and set up shop in another area of the city. In our impaired state, we had come to the conclusion that we would be better off without Miko.

The next day, Miko dropped off the sack we had planned to steal—and steal it we did. But instead of selling it and pocketing the money, we smoked it up with some people that Kevin knew. Once all of the rocks were gone and my high had subsided, I realized that I didn't have anywhere to go but back to the 'hood. It was the biggest mistake of my young life.

I spent the day trying to duck Miko, but there was no getting away from him. When he caught up with me, he was in the car with two of his goons, and he ordered me to get in. Even though I was high and afraid, I was able to think quick on my feet, so when Miko asked me where I'd been and what happened to the dope, I lied and told him that the police had raided the spot and taken me to the youth home. I even told him that he could take me to my mother's place and ask her, because she was the one who had gotten me out that morning. To my surprise, Miko took me up on the offer, putting the car in drive and speeding off toward my mother's house.

I sat in the back of the car, terrified. My mother had no idea what was going on in my life. What would she think if I showed up with a drug kingpin and two of his goons? As we drove toward her house, I realized that I didn't have the nerve to go through with my plan. I had no idea what they would do to my mother, and I wasn't about to jeopardize my family because of my bullshit.

So I cracked. I came clean, telling Miko that I had smoked up the sack.

Miko was shocked. He had known for a while that the other guys had been fucking around with our stash, but he never suspected that I would join in. In so many ways, I was still a child, and it never occurred to him that I would try some bullshit like this. Miko's goons, however, didn't seem surprised. They didn't care about me being a skinny fourteen-year-old who was just months removed from living with his mother—they were street-hardened veterans who no longer felt empathy, and they were all too eager to make an example out of me.

Miko had no choice but to let them do it. He was bound by the code of the streets, and he knew that the moment he made an exception to the code, word would get out that he had gone soft.

They took me to the house on Maiden, where one of Miko's goons grabbed me by the back of my shirt and dragged me inside. I pleaded with Miko, promising that I would work off the money I had stolen. All of it, every dollar. But my promise meant nothing to him. He leaned down to look in my face and said, "How you gonna work off a sack when you a crackhead?"

Those words hit me harder than the beating I was about to take. They forced me to see the true face of the situation: that I had become the thing I despised—a consumer of the poison I had once taken pride in selling to others.

As soon as we reached the living room, Miko turned around and punched me in the face. I staggered backward, and before I could regain my composure, one of his goons joined in, punching me in the back of the head. I did my best to fight back, but my adolescent strength was no match for that of two grown men. Miko's goons quickly overpowered me and administered a thorough beatdown. By the time Miko stopped them, I was lying in a pool of blood.

As I lay there, I thought I was going to die. My nose was pouring blood, and the entire left side of my face was swollen. It was hard for me to breathe. Miko told me to get up from the floor, clean myself up, and wait at the house for them to come back. I looked at his goons in a haze of confusion, thinking about the rifle in the back room. But I knew I didn't have the heart to shoot anyone.

All of this was my fault. I was the one who smoked the sack—the one who thought I could pull one over on my boss. But, even though I knew Miko had held back on the beating, I felt betrayed. I had looked up to him as a big brother, but when it came down to it, I was nothing more than a laborer to him. A deep wound pressed itself into my psyche. The way I saw it, if Miko could turn on me, then anyone could turn on me. In that moment, I made a silent vow to kill the next person to put his or her hands on me.

I stumbled to the bathroom and stared at myself in the mirror. My lips were swollen and cracked, and my eye had a lump the size of a plum beneath it. I felt lonely and vulnerable, but as much as I wanted to cry, I couldn't. I didn't know what to do or where to turn, and I was afraid that Miko and his goons would return at any minute and finish beating me until I died. But a few minutes after that thought crossed my mind, I heard them exit the house.

I slumped to the bathroom floor and curled into a tight ball. Thoughts of my mother and father tumbled through my mind. I thought about everything they had told me about God and how none of it made sense in that moment. I cursed their blond-haired, blue-eyed God. How could he allow this to happen to me? I wondered. Where were the caring, protective arms of Jesus when I needed him? Where were my mother and father while I was lying on the pissy bathroom floor of a crack house?

The sound of someone coming from upstairs made me pull myself up from the floor. My face was throbbing, and each time I took a breath, it felt like I had been stabbed in my side. I was standing at the sink, rinsing the blood from my mouth, when I heard a soft voice asking if I was all right.

I looked up to see a woman named Sharon who lived upstairs with her one-year-old son, and I nodded my head to indicate that I was okay. Sharon looked at me with pity. She grabbed a cloth to wash my face with cold water, and as she did so, she told me that I needed to get out of the game and leave Miko alone. A deep sense of shame and embarrassment overtook me, and I resented Sharon for it—but I knew she was right.

THE NEXT MORNING, I was knocking on the door of my sister Tamica's house. When she opened the door and saw my face, she burst into tears. She said she wanted to find Miko and beat his ass. Tamica and I had grown up fighting side by side; no matter who she got into it with, I was right there with her, and she never hesitated to return the favor. I told her the details of what had happened (leaving out the part about me smoking laced joints), and she told me I could stay with her as long as I needed. It wasn't home, but after months of fighting to survive on my own in the streets, here was a chance to start anew.

But already the pathological behavior of the drug trade had seeped into my soul. I had been given a chance to change, but in a matter of days, I would go back to my old ways.

8

The day of my sentencing, I carried a picture of Brenda and me to the holding room outside of the courtroom. There were about fifteen of us there, and as I sat down, my attention was drawn to a light-skinned inmate with a long ponytail who had just come into the bullpen. I couldn't place who he was, but I felt like I knew him. I watched him as he scanned the graffiti-filled steel and concrete holding cell.

Then he asked a question to the room. "What do y'all think the judge will do to a man serving a life sentence if he raped another inmate?" He looked around for an answer.

A few guys replied that there wasn't much the judge could do if someone was already serving a life sentence. After considering their answers, the guy who had asked the question told them that he had asked it because that's the situation he was in.

Immediately I knew he was Seven, the guy that my bunky had told me about. He didn't look like the kind of guy who'd be capable of raping another man, or at least he didn't fit my picture of Seven. I had imagined him as a bald-headed brute foaming at the mouth with scars covering his face, but he looked just like anyone else.

A few minutes passed, and I was called to stand before the county judge for sentencing.

I was nineteen years old.

WHEN I ENTERED the courtroom, I saw my parents, Brenda, and my ex-girlfriend Nycci from Ohio sitting in the second row. I gave them a smile, but my heart was as burdened as it had ever felt. I couldn't take the pain of seeing the last people on earth who I knew loved me, so I turned back around to face the judge.

I didn't know what to expect from the sentencing. My lawyer had assured me that I was looking at no more than ten years. He said the judge would be lenient because of my age and the fact that I had been shot a couple of years earlier, so I took his advice when he said I should plead guilty. While I wasn't excited about doing the next ten years in prison, I had seen guys get sentenced to forty, fifty, and sixty years for similar charges. Ten years wasn't nothing, but it was a trip to the beach compared to fifty years or life behind bars.

I wasn't an idiot. I had a GED, and I had done well in school—but I had a hard time understanding the subtleties of the law as it applied to my plea agreement. It was my understanding that my lawyer had already made the deal to get me ten years, but when I approached the bench, the judge informed me that there was no preexisting sentence agreement in place, and I could be sentenced to any number of years, including life.

There were so many emotions and thoughts running through my head. I was still a child, and everything about the legal system was intimidating, so instead of trying to buy time or take my case to trial, I went along with the program. I pled guilty.

"Mr. White," the judge said, "it is the court's understanding that you will enter a no-contest plea to the charge of murder in the second degree."

He looked up at me from a stack of papers. "You do understand that this means you are forfeiting your right to a bench trial or trial by a jury of your peers. And that you are agreeing to be sentenced to any number of years up to life in prison by this judge." I nodded.

He then asked if I had anything to say, and I told him I did. I apologized to the victim's family and asked them to forgive me for what I had done to their loved one. I then asked the judge for leniency.

After I was done speaking, the judge looked down at the sentencing guidelines. I could hear deep breathing behind me and the sound of someone nervously tapping a foot on the floor. In that moment, I was too terrified to note how strange it was that my life and future were being determined by a set of calculations on a piece of paper.

The judge finished with his calculations and looked back up at me. "In the matter of James White, it is the court's decision that Mr. White shall be sentenced to serve two years for felony firearm possession, and fifteen to forty years for murder in the second degree, to be served consecutively in the Michigan Department of Corrections."

My knees buckled. I couldn't believe this was happening. I had hardly begun to live. I couldn't even comprehend the thought of spending two, maybe even four, decades of my life behind bars. My shoulders slumped forward as I lowered my head, and I could hear my mother and Brenda crying behind me. I was too afraid to turn around and face them. Instead, I turned and walked toward the door, with the bailiff leading me back to the bullpen.

When I stepped into the bullpen, everyone went silent. They hadn't heard what happened in the courtroom, but they could tell from my reaction that it was serious.

I sat back down on the bench where I had left my bag and rested my head against the wall. My eyes felt like they were going to burst. Slowly, I began shutting down my mind, shutting out the memories of everything that used to make me happy in life. I no longer wanted to think of the things that used to be; I had a sentence to serve, and I couldn't afford to be distracted by thoughts of everything I had lost.

As I sat there mentally deleting the files from my past, my lawyer called me to the visiting booth. He told me about my appeal and my rights, but he might as well have been explaining the blueprints to the Great Wall of China. My sadness was already giving way to a deep, dark anger that made it impossible to think about anything else. Fortunately, no one in the bullpen asked me any questions, because my reaction would have left me with even more charges to face.

After a minute of staring at the floor, I looked to my left and noticed Seven luring a white guy into the small bathroom area inside the bullpen. Evil and perversity dripped from his pores like sweat, and it sickened me to know that I would be spending the next seventeen years of my life around men like him.

TWO DAYS LATER, I was transferred upstate to Riverside Correctional Facility, where the state of Michigan quarantined all prisoners under the age of twenty-one. It was a two-and-a-half-hour ride from Detroit to Ionia, and when we finally pulled up to the prison, my heart started pounding. The concertina-wired fences looked menacing, like spiraling rows of teeth that were hungry for tender flesh. We circled the parking lot for a minute before pulling through a checkpoint at the front of the prison. The deputies checked their pistols, then came around to the back of the van to order us out. We climbed down and shuffled away from the van, stretching our legs as the guards funneled us inside the building.

One of the first things I noticed was how neatly manicured the lawns were outside. The prison stood in stark contrast to the dilapidated schools that sat like scabs across Detroit's decaying landscape. It wasn't until years later that I understood the politics of it all. It was almost as if the state was more willing to invest money in the upkeep of prisons than in schools.

The intake process at Riverside was similar to the one at the county jail. We were forced to strip out of our personal clothes and stand around ass-naked in front of more people than I had ever known in my entire nineteen years on earth. It was through this process that I started to become detached from my own body. I no longer felt like I belonged to myself.

After being dressed out in state blues, we were called up one by one to the desk where an officer waited. When I got there, she asked me my name and told me that I was now prisoner number 219184, urging me to remember that number like I remembered my own name. I thought about her words as I filed over to the next window to retrieve my state-issued clothing.

At orientation, an officer told us how prison worked and gave us a list of dos and don'ts. He told us if we violated the rules, we would be locked down in our cells or placed in the hole. He told us to never gamble, borrow money, or engage in homosexual sex, and he also cautioned us against playing basketball. He said that all of these things were hotbeds for conflict.

Some of us, he said, would do easy time; others would mess up and get in a bunch of trouble. Some, he said, wouldn't make it at all. He didn't explain what he meant by that, but it wouldn't be long before I learned exactly what he was talking about.

IN MY CELL that night, I stood at the window, staring out at the darkening sky. A few panes of glass were missing from the window, and I could feel the cool fall air blowing in from outside. A deep sadness gripped me as I thought about how badly I had messed up my life. I couldn't stop thinking about the two children I would be leaving behind. My daughter from the previous relationship was now five months old, and Brenda was about five months pregnant. It was extremely painful to know I had helped bring two lives into the world but would be unable to care for and nurture them.

I started talking to God and asking him why he had allowed this to happen to me. I couldn't make any sense of the deep pit of darkness I had fallen into. Every bad thing that ever happened to me came floating back as I stared out at the sky. I started feeling sorry for myself, but that feeling soon turned to anger. I got angry with God. I got angry at my parents, my teachers, and everyone else I felt had let me down. I felt unlovable, like no one cared enough about me to wonder why I had veered so far off the path. Never once did I stop to think about how much I had let myself down. As my anger grew, I looked out my cell window and noticed several alley cats sniffing around a garbage can near the back of the main chow hall. In that moment, I would have given anything to be one of them, picking through the garbage, but free to roam the world.

IN THE MONTHS that followed, my social circle remained small. It was difficult being alone in prison, but I would rather do my time alone than deal with guys who were fake or who didn't share my values. More important, I was trying to figure out how to get home to my family.

I missed everything about home, and I tried to connect with my father and Brenda whenever I could. The hardest conversation was the first time that I called my father from prison. In the middle of our call, he broke down crying, and I was at a loss for words. It was the first time that I realized I had hurt my father deeply. I could only imagine what it was like for him, having to explain to his friends that his son was in prison and would be there for nearly two decades, or longer. He told me that he and my stepmother were going to come up and see me soon, and then we hung up. Georgia and Brenda were planning to come see me as well, so for the next couple of days, I focused on my upcoming visits, pacing my cell floor each night in anticipation of getting a little piece of home.

During the day, I read whatever novels I could get my hands on. I had even started reading the Bible. I mostly read the stories that I thought fit my situation (like Job's), but I wasn't gaining the sense of peace that I desired. So I put the Bible down and focused on the escape that novels provided.

One day, I was mopping the floor when an officer called me into his office and told me to get ready because I had a visit. I was bursting with excitement as I walked back down to my cell. I went into the bathroom and freshened up, then headed to the visiting room. When I set eyes on Brenda, a deep sense of longing overcame me. She looked radiant with the baby showing, and her smile was beautiful and comforting. We embraced and kissed each other tenderly, as though it was our first time. She placed my hand on her stomach when the baby started kicking, and I felt a surge of guilt shoot through my body. Brenda looked so vulnerable and there was nothing I could do to be there for her.

Brenda and Georgia caught me up on what was happening back in the 'hood. We talked about the baby and its due date. Brenda said that she wanted to marry me when I came home and assured me that she would always be there for me. I listened to her, but emotionally I was shutting down the part of me that would have hoped on that possibility. I knew she wouldn't be able to handle the pressure of being there for me over the long haul, and I didn't want to open myself up to the pain of thinking about it. Little did I know how true that intuition would prove to be. As it turned out, that visit would be the last time I'd see her during my incarceration.

The following week, I got a second visit from my family. My father brought my stepmother, stepbrother, two younger sisters, and Brenda along with him, but Brenda wasn't allowed to come in because of an issue with her ID. My father told me that she was in the lobby crying, but she would be all right. He said she told him to tell me that she loved me.

We spent the visit talking about how I was adjusting to prison. As we talked, I stared at my young siblings and was struck by just how badly I had failed them as a big brother.

My younger sister Nakia looked up at me and asked me some of the questions I feared. "Bro, are you all right? What is it like in there?" Her questions were innocent, yet loaded. Behind those seemingly simple questions was a whole lot of fear, and I now understand why this was the case. When someone gets locked up, so does their family.

When the visit was over, I went straight back to my cell. I didn't want to talk to anyone because I wanted to hold on to every morsel of that visit for as long as I could. I wanted the smell of my family to cling to my nostrils for as long as possible, I wanted to hold on to the feeling of their touch. It was the only reminder I had of my own humanity.

9

EAST MARGARET STREET
Detroit, Michigan
1986

Tamica's place was the perfect setup for me. Her building had a built-in clientele, with addicts occupying nearly every apartment on all three floors. Once our neighbors knew I had a sack, all I had to do was sit in front of the building and serve them as they hustled up whatever money they could. I had stopped smoking the laced joints, and within weeks, the money was rolling in. I could feel my swagger coming back.

I went shopping down in Highland Park and came back with some fly Ballys, a handful of silk shirts, and a couple of outfits from Guess. I started hanging around the corner on a street named Savannah, where all the neighborhood girls would go. They adored me, no doubt because I was generous with my ill-gotten capital, and their attention made me feel like a 'hood celebrity.

Tamica's neighborhood was right down the street from Palmer Park, which was prime real estate for drugs and prostitution. The transvestites who hung out in the park spent hundreds, sometimes thousands, of dollars a day. My friends from Savannah would hang out at a nearby restaurant called Ted's, and we would laugh as we watched streams of balding white men roam up and down Woodward, trying to find themselves a transvestite or crack whore. Most of them drove luxury sedans and had traveled there from the suburbs.

This was one of the 'hood's many contradictions. Affluent white men were free to come into our community to buy drugs and sex as they pleased. If they got pulled over for soliciting, more often than not they were given a slap on the wrist and returned to the safety of the suburbs. But for us, the parks we had once played in as children were no longer safe, and the streets that had once been a source of pride were now forgotten cesspools that the city would rather forget. I continued selling over the course of that year, and things were beginning to look promising. My two older brothers had come up from Chicago, and we began flipping sacks together. Soon, I moved with my brother Alan back to our old neighborhood. Alan's girlfriend also moved up with their daughter, making our house feel like a home for the first time I could remember. It wasn't long, however, before the brutality of the streets reared its ugly head again.

One day, we were all standing outside kicking it when a female named Pig came running down the street, screaming and crying. She told us that her cousin Shannon Bell had been shot and killed.

Damn, I thought. *I was just talking to him the other day.* I hadn't seen Shannon much since our days in elementary school, but we ran into each other on Glenfield from time to time and would hang out whenever he came to visit Pig and her sister. Now he was gone, shot dead at the tender age of fifteen. Detroit was experiencing another long, bloody year, so we weren't surprised when the violence claimed someone we knew. But in the back of our minds, we all had the same lingering questions: *Who's gonna be next?* and *How soon will it be?*

We never expressed this fear out loud, but our body language spoke for us. Our movements were tense. Our eyes became alert when strangers approached us, and we reacted impulsively to any potential threat. Clearly, the stakes had been raised.

The 'hood was at war with itself, turning its anger inward like a bloodthirsty cannibal. It destroyed life and left in its wake a stream of torn families, abandoned children, and a vicious cycle of gun violence. No one deserves to see their homies die at such a young age, but that was our reality, and it desensitized us to the good and joy that life could offer. I grew colder inside—if you were cold, at least it meant you weren't weak.

I no longer cared if I lived or died. In fact, I started looking forward to the day of my demise. It was a twisted thought, but it gave me a sense of control. If I embraced death, then I wouldn't have to live in fear of dying—at least that's what I told myself. The reality was that my true fear was of *living*, because living had become too painful. Around each corner, I saw a bullet with my name on it. In every car that sped by, I saw a death machine chauffeured by the grim reaper himself.

I knew that it was only a matter of time before I would have to kill or be killed. If I was quick on the draw, it would be the former. But if not, I would join the hundreds of young men and women who were lost in the war that rages through our community. How can a child expect to exist like this and not go insane?

ONE NIGHT TOWARD the end of summer, I was sitting in the living room when I heard loud noises coming from our front porch.

When I looked out of the window, I noticed a man with a gun pointed at my brother Alan's head. Alan's girlfriend stood nearby with her hands in the air.

I immediately leapt into action. I grabbed a pistol out of the closet, ran out of the back door, and then circled the house. Rounding the front corner, I hollered for the gunman to back away from my brother. As soon as he saw me, he pushed Alan and took off running. I squeezed off several shots as he disappeared around the corner.

My brother and his girl were unharmed, and the gunman had gotten away. But my heart was pounding from fear and excitement. It was the first time I had fired a gun at another human being.

Not long after that, Alan decided to relocate to the West Side, to a neighborhood called Brightmoor. Before he moved, he told one of his old friends that she and her daughters could share the house with me, and she became somewhat of a guardian. But my behavior didn't change under her watch—I continued drinking and sexing and dealing drugs until, finally, my brother Art told me that I needed to move off of Glenfield. He was tired of coming over and seeing the house full of weed smoke, noise, and teenagers trying to act like they were grown.

I thought I was ready to get my life back on track, so I called my father and let him know that I wanted to come home.

10

MICHIGAN REFORMATORY
Ionia, Michigan
October 1991

Thirty days after I completed quarantine, the state transferred me and a motley crew of other inmates to the Michigan Reformatory. The place was known by the name "Gladiator School," a reference to the Roman Colosseum, where fights to the death were held for people's entertainment. At MR, stabbings were a daily occurrence, we were told, and other vicious acts of brutality were as much a part of the culture as the putrid slop they served in the chow line.

As our prison van drove up, the high, gray walls surrounding this antiquated behemoth of a prison stamped out any thoughts of freedom. In its place, we felt only fear.

Not that we showed it. To break the tension, we joked with the one white guy who had made the trip with us. Kevin was one of the few white guys who were cool enough to hang with our little circle. All too often in prison, suburban white guys tried to emulate the swagger of hip-hop artists, and it made the other inmates want to put them to the test. The ones who had the least trouble were those who didn't try to be anyone other than themselves, and this was the case with Kevin. He was down-to-earth and had a crazy sense of humor.

In the processing room, as we waited our turns, we joked that Kevin should stick with us so the booty bandits wouldn't get him. He told us to fuck off. We should stick with him, he said, because he could whop all of our asses. Everyone laughed.

Finally, I was given my assignment: Cell I-80, which was close to the middle of the rock on the inside of the cellblock. There were two main blocks at the Reformatory, each five stories tall. On each tier, the inside faced the prison yard, and the outside faced those big gray walls.

At the door of my cell, I looked down the tier. It seemed to stretch on into infinity.

I stepped inside and instantly became nauseous. The place smelled like raw sewage had been dumped on the floor. The hard, green, plastic-covered mattress was peeling and cracked, and the pillow was as flat as a pancake. The faucet at the sink dripped brown liquid, and the toilet was full of human waste. I held my nose and reached to flush the toilet, praying that it wouldn't overflow. It didn't. But I was soon to learn that the Reformatory's hundred-year-old plumbing didn't actually work. When you flushed your toilet, the waste would routinely show up in someone else's. Nearly every morning, I was awakened by the smell of someone's bowel movement floating in my toilet like an uninvited guest.

I walked out onto the yard with the guys from intake. The sun cut through the crisp fall air, but on the ground more than a thousand black and brown men surged back and forth. I had never been in a place that housed so many people.

We stood out from the rest of the inmates because we were still wearing the blue jackets we had been given in quarantine. (Inmates who were able bought clothes from one of the MDOC-approved catalogues, or had them sent from home—a small way of expressing uniqueness in an environment where you're seen as just a number.)

The veteran inmates were in full predator mode, searching our faces to find who among us was weak enough to be considered prey. It wasn't long before we saw a couple of guys walking off with Kevin in tow, arms draped around his shoulders. All we could do was watch helplessly. We were on enemy terrain, and at the end of the day, there was nothing we could do to save him.

Later that night, when we were back in our cells, I was awakened by the sound of jingling keys as several officers and nurses ran down the rock. I strained to see as far down the tier as I could, and the rest of the guys grew quiet as we listened to hear what was going on. After nearly an hour, the officers and nurses came back, rolling a gurney down the tier with a body on it. A white sheet was draped across the inmate's face, and we later learned that it was Kevin. By the time we came out for chow, word had spread throughout the prison that Kevin had committed suicide.

Then on my way to breakfast the next morning, I witnessed my first stabbing. A group of us were taking the back steps down to the chow hall when a slim, dark-skinned brother slid past us, stabbed a guy several times in the neck, and calmly discarded the shank in the mailbox at the bottom of the steps. The victim clutched his neck and took off running back up the stairs. By the time we reached the walkway that led to the chow hall, officers were running into the building.

I stayed up late that night, looking around the cell for something I could make into a shank. This was a skill I would come to perfect over the years. A plastic bottle became a tool to be melted down and sharpened to a point that was sharp enough to take out an eye or puncture a lung. In the bakery, the carts that we used to cool fresh-baked bread became smorgasbords of high-quality steel shanks, and a whisk could be turned into a dozen or so ice picks. If I got my hands on a crude piece of metal, you could be sure that I would turn it into a tool of violence.

Over the next couple of months, I witnessed one act of bloodshed after another, and I knew it wouldn't be long before I was sucked into the chaos of the big yard. Gladiator School was living up to its name.

WITHIN A FEW weeks, most of the guys I had transferred in with were sent to other prisons. We weren't yet seasoned convicts, so the administration saw it fit to send us to the newer correctional facilities. Several went to Brooks, located in Muskegon. I was sent to a prison in Carson City.

The prison sat on a sprawling piece of land that contained two prisons and a farm, on the other side of the gate. The lawns had been landscaped by inmates, and the new buildings looked like school buildings or recreation centers compared to the old, castle-like fortress I had just left. Each unit was outfitted with microwaves, a pool table, and a universal weight machine. The food was better, and they gave us access to the gym and at least four hours in the yard every day. Overall, the inmates appeared to be less hostile than those at the Reformatory, and more optimistic.

It was a nice place, but in many ways, that made things worse by giving us the illusion that we would be treated better by the staff. By creating a more livable environment, the state was creating more docile inmates. This worked well for those who became complacent when given the extra amenities, but I hadn't been locked up long enough to be pacified; I was still angry at the system. Whenever I disobeyed the orders of officers or got into heated exchanges with other inmates, the officers would ask older inmates to talk to me. The older inmates would come ask me to be cool so that I wouldn't get myself in trouble. One inmate could mess it up for the rest of them, they said.

But instead of taking their advice, I felt insulted. Who did these guys think they were? They worked harder for the administration than they did for themselves, and they would put up with anything from the guards so long as they had their microwaves and more time in the yard. I appreciated these conveniences, but I damn well wasn't trying to get comfortable.

I STARTED OFF in 5-Block, which had single-man cells. It was a unit for predators and inmates with behavioral problems; however, they would put anyone in 5 if they didn't have space in the other units. For the first two weeks, I kept mostly to myself, and the only person that I talked to on a regular basis was a brother named O'Neal-El.

One day, he told me that he was trying to finish a book he had been writing. I asked him what it was about, and he told me he was writing about his neighborhood. O'Neal-El was a member of the infamous drug crew Young Boys Incorporated, and his book was a collection of stories loosely based on his experience in the streets. He asked if I wanted to read one of his stories, and I laughed at the idea of an inmate writing a book. But I didn't have anything else to do, so I said yes.

When I started reading O'Neal-El's stories, I couldn't put them down. The stories were only eighty or ninety pages long, but they were detailed and vivid. When I finished, I felt like I had grown up alongside O'Neal-El and his crew, wearing Adidas Top Tens, fur-lined Max Julien coats, and wide-brimmed campaign hats.

When I told O'Neal-El this, he said I should go to the library and check out a book by Donald Goines. So I sent a request over and asked to be placed on a callout (an approved time period for inmates to be in a specific area) for the library. The next week, my request was approved, and I found myself in the library, ask-ing the clerk if she had any Donald Goines books. She pointed me to a separate room, which was filled with books by Black au-thors. Upon entering the room, I checked the shelf for and found a Goines novel titled *Eldorado Red*.

I brought the book to the clerk for checkout, and she gave me a form to sign that said I would be charged five dollars if I lost the book or it got stolen. The only books we were required to fill out these forms for were ones written by Black authors. I mumbled to myself about racism as I looked around the room for other books that might interest me.

The room was full of volumes by unfamiliar names—Marcus Garvey, Ivan Van Sertima, and Cheikh Anta Diop—but I knew there had to be something to them, because they were in the same room as Donald Goines. I thumbed through a few. They might as well have been written in Sanskrit, because I had no clue what words like "revolution," "colonialism," or "repatriate" meant.

I slid the books back on the shelf and returned to the main area of the library, gathering up a few more novels and bringing them to the desk for checkout. The clerk promised that they would hold a few Donald Goines novels for me to pick up later.

When I got back to my cell, it was nearing time for count, so I sat down and opened up the dog-eared pages of *Eldorado Red*. From the first page, I was hooked. Goines's vivid tale of inner-city life and the underground lottery had me in its spell, and his ability to articulate the pain of the streets validated the anger, frustration, and disappointment I felt toward life in the 'hood. Goines placed me back on the streets of Detroit; he made me feel alive again. I read the whole thing that night.

By the time my next callout came, I nearly ran to the library, and when I got there, it was as though the clerks had known I was coming. They had watched other inmates become intoxicated by Donald's work, and they knew I would be back. They smiled as they handed over *Dopefiend* and *Whoreson,* the books they had reserved for me. I took the books in my hand as though they were the Holy Grail and rushed back to my cell, where I proceeded to read through the day and late into the night. By the time I lay down at three in the morning, my eyes burned with the strain. But I couldn't wait for sunlight so that I could keep indulging what was fast becoming my deepest passion.

The following week, I was transferred to a unit where the cells were double-bunked. My bunky went by the name Murder, which seemed funny to me at the time, because he must have weighed 140 pounds soaking wet. We hit it off immediately. He was originally from Chicago, but had family on the East Side of Detroit, where I had grown up.

Murder and I found different ways to ensure that we each had some alone time in the cell—an arrangement that keeps bunkies from getting on each other's nerves. When we were in the cell together, Murder would usually watch television while I read. He wasn't into sports as much as I was, and the only movies he seemed to enjoy were old westerns, none of which appealed to me at the time.

Outside of reading, music was my main means of escape. I was raised in a household where, over the course of one day, you would hear my parents, aunts, and uncles playing artists as diverse as Anita Baker, Pink Floyd, Luther Vandross, Prince, and Parliament Funkadelic. When rap entered my small world, I was hooked, and I killed a lot of time in prison by sitting in the dayroom listening to other inmates as they freestyled and recited the lyrics from their favorite rappers.

It was during one of these sessions that I met a tall, gangly brother who went by the name DJ X. He had a deep, raspy voice and would rap nonstop while beating on his chest. One day, he began using a bunch of names that I wasn't familiar with, like Huey P. Newton, George Jackson, and Malcolm X. I had heard a few of their names while listening to X Clan and Public Enemy, but I didn't have a working knowledge of who they were.

When DJ X was done rapping, I asked him about the names he had mentioned. He stared at me with an incredulous look on his face. He couldn't believe that I didn't know about Nat Turner, Assata Shakur, and the other men and women he had mentioned in his song. I assured him that I was ignorant, and he suggested that I check out *The Autobiography of Malcolm X* the next time I made a trip to the library.

WHEN I PICKED up Malcolm X's autobiography, the picture of an intelligent-looking man in horn-rimmed glasses seemed familiar. I had noticed a few brothers wearing T-shirts with Malcolm's image on the front, and I had also seen in the news that Spike Lee was making a movie based on the book, but I hadn't stopped long enough to discover what all the hoopla was about. All I knew was that white people appeared to be upset about the movie—as upset as they had gotten when a school named after Malcolm X had opened up in Detroit.

As the pieces started coming together in my mind, I got the feeling that Malcolm X had to be a serious gangster. (I mean, you have to admit that there's a badass sound to the name Malcolm X.) But when I read the back cover of the book, I felt disappointed.

The synopsis made it sound like I was about to read another in a long list of stories about Black people who *just wanted to get along*. I had grown tired of hearing about Martin Luther King's "I Have a Dream" speech and the story of Rosa Parks on the bus. To me, these stories only served two purposes: one, to make white people feel guilt-free, and two, to appease Black people and ensure that they remained docile in their attempts to get equal respect. But despite my apprehension, I decided to go ahead and read the book. Without question, it was one of the best and most important decisions I have ever made.

Donald Goines's novels had created in me a desire to read, but Malcolm's words snatched my eyes open and embedded in me a burning desire to do something meaningful with my life. His ability to go from a common street thug to a world-renowned orator and scholar inspired me in a way that nothing had before.

Once I had read Malcolm, I began reading with a purpose. I devoured everything from political science to erotica to contemporary fiction and philosophy—but the most important objects of my study were books of Black history, as told by people of African descent.

My reading of Black history gave me a sense of pride and dignity that I didn't have prior to coming to prison. I learned about African kingdoms like Mali, Ashanti, and Timbuktu through classic works by the scholars Chancellor Williams, Cheikh Anta Diop, Dr. Yosef Ben Jochannan, and J. A. Rogers. I learned that my ancestors were more than passive observers of history; they were in fact an integral part of the development of civilization as we know it today. I discovered our great contributions to the world, and it was a shot in the arm for my self-worth. It also helped me understand why the majority of the prison population looked like me and why there were so many deep-rooted racial antagonisms inside of prison.

In school, we hadn't learned about freedom fighters like Nat

Turner, Toussaint-Louverture, Ann Nzingha, Assata Shakur, Malcolm X, and Huey P. Newton. The things we learned about Black history seemed designed to keep us dreaming of a better tomorrow, one that would only come when white America felt sorry enough to treat us as equals. This never sat well with me and, for the most part, left me feeling angry, inferior, and confused.

The more I read Malcolm X's autobiography, the more things started to make sense to me. Coming into prison, I was confused about religion. I had long ago given up the blond-haired, blue-eyed version of Jesus, whom my mother worshipped and had raised us to believe in. When we went to church or Sunday school, we were discouraged from raising critical questions and told to take anything the preacher and the Bible said at face value.

Anytime I found myself in serious trouble, I would pray to Jesus and ask him to pull me out of the mess. My motivation wasn't to establish a real relationship with God—it was to get my ass out of hot water. But that didn't mean that a small part of me didn't desire a sincere spiritual connection to the source of all life.

Malcolm's autobiography was the first book to make me question the faith in which I had been raised. His insights into how Christianity had been used to make African people passive in the face of such horrendous treatment by slave masters made me look at things differently. I started to question why all of the characters in the Bible were depicted as white when we saw them at church. I wanted to know where all the Black people were in the Bible. I knew we hadn't just fallen from the sky, but when I asked other Christians, I was either met with a blank stare or told it didn't matter, that God wasn't a color. It was the politically correct thing for them to say, but they said it nervously, suggesting that they knew differently. The fact is, color does matter—especially when you're looking for evidence that God cares about people like you.

The more disenchanted I became with Christianity, the more intrigued I became with Islam. From the time I was a child, I had envisioned a world that was all-inclusive and a God that was all-loving, regardless of color. Malcolm's experience in Mecca and his description of Islam as a religion that didn't discriminate made me feel good, so I began researching the Islamic organizations in prison, looking for one to join.

At the time, there were four dominant Islamic groups in the prisons of Michigan: the Sunni Muslim sect, which holds traditional Islamic beliefs; the Nation of Islam, which has strong Black nationalist views and follows the teachings of the Honorable Elijah Muhammad and Minister Farrakhan; the Moorish Science Temple of America, which follows the teachings of Prophet Noble Drew Ali; and finally, the Melanic Islamic Palace of the Rising Sun. The Melanics profess a militant Afrocentric ideology, and it was for this reason that they drew my interest. I was impressed by the discipline and cultural perspective of the few members I had encountered, and I admired the red, black, and green badge that they wore, because it reminded me of X Clan and other rappers that I loved.

The Melanics used the Bible and the Quran as their spiritual books of choice, but not exclusively so. Members were encouraged to read other religious texts and drink from the many streams that our ancestors had used to quench their thirst for spiritual rejuvenation. It wasn't uncommon for a Melanic spiritual advisor to quote *David Walker's Appeal* or George Jackson's *Blood in My Eye* during a sermon, then turn to a passage in the Bible or a surah in the Quran. Instead of trying to dazzle us with an imaginary paradise or the terrifying threat of eternal damnation, the spiritual advisors set out to help us understand our daily realities. This approach reminded me of Malcolm, and how instead of standing at the podium as though he were on the mountaintop, he came down and walked among the people. He related to their struggle, pain, and frustration because he had lived it himself.

In prison, there was a negative stigma attached to the guys

who attended Muslim services. The administration didn't like the unity and saw the Muslim brotherhoods as covers for gang activity. On top of that, the more predatory inmates didn't like how the brotherhoods provided a safe haven for some of the more vulnerable guys. Muslims have a reputation of sticking together and taking care of their members' problems, not unlike any other family, where the individual's problem becomes the problem of the group. Unfortunately, however, there are inmates who take advantage of this dynamic. Some need protection, others are opportunists who seize the chance to have their basic needs met, and others are in search of the acceptance they didn't get from their own family.

Because of this stigma, I was very careful about my decision to attend Melanic services. But after reading several more books and talking with more of the members, I decided to check out one of their Saturday morning services.

It was unlike anything I had ever experienced in a church. The brothers wore neatly pressed blues, black fezzes, and polished shoes. The podium was decorated with a large flag and a picture of Nat Turner, who I would later learn was the organization's prophet. At the beginning of the service, while prayer was being held, the brothers stood until they were given instruction to be seated. The brothers stationed at the door wore stoic expressions as they directed guests to their seats at the front of the room.

We stood as the program began. The brothers formed a ten-man prayer pyramid, moving in a counterclockwise motion and calling out to our ancestors. I was impressed by the precision of their movements. It was an awesome display of power, respect, and spirituality. In an uncompromising display of solidarity, the brothers paid homage to those who had come before us while praising the Creator for a chance to do something meaningful with our lives.

After that first service, the brothers asked me if I would come back and visit again. I told them that I wouldn't make any promises, but I'd consider it. I visited over the next couple of months, but only sporadically. (This was mostly because I was spending most nights reading until two or three o'clock in the morning, and the last thing I wanted to do was get up at seven o'clock in the morning to get ready for service.) Despite this conflict, I kept reading books of Black history and building my relationship with the brothers.

MY SPIRITUAL AND intellectual growth was one of the most important things that had ever happened to me. But that winter, as I sat counting away the days in prison, something even more important was manifesting in my life.

It was late December, and Brenda's due date was approaching. It had been a few months since I saw her last, and we had only been talking occasionally. The cost of phone calls had long ago taken their toll, and Georgia couldn't afford to pay for us to speak on a daily basis. Brenda did what she could to help with the phone bill, and I did my best not to call too much.

But on January 7, 1992, I stepped outside of the unit for some fresh air and fought through the frosty winter air to dial Georgia's number. When Georgia answered the phone, her voice cascaded over the line like the music of a symphony, and I knew that my son had been born into the world. As I listened intently, my eyes watered with tears that froze as soon as they hit the air. I was happy to hear that he had been born healthy and that Brenda decided to name him after me, but my chest felt like I had swallowed a cinder block. It hurt like hell knowing that I wouldn't be there to guide my son through life.

I was terrified that my son would get caught up in the cycle of violence, drugs, and crime that had claimed so many from my generation—including me. I didn't want him to join the long line of young Black males who became statistics, and the more I thought about it, the angrier I became.

When I returned to my cell, I lay on my bunk and thought about my son. I imagined what he looked like. I wondered which characteristics he had inherited from me and which ones he had inherited from his mother. Brenda was a beautiful young lady, and I thought I was a decent-looking brother, so I was pretty sure that our son would be a looker. As I thought about him, my heart began filling with an unbelievable joy. I knew I had to find a way to be a part of my son's life.

I vowed to find a way to be a father, even though I was in prison. This meant that I had to change my thinking. There could be no more settling for less in life. I could no longer think destructively about other Black males, and I could no longer justify shooting, beating, or selling drugs to those who looked like me. I had to reclaim my humanity and soften my heart so that I could be a voice of reason and wisdom for my boy.

I knew that "nigga" in me had to be subdued by the African warrior I was destined to become. I had given up on myself, my parents, and my brothers and sisters—but I would be damned if I'd give up on my children. I was determined to fight against the side of me that didn't think I could be anything more than a thuggish criminal or a predator to my community. I knew I was in for the fight of my life, but I was prepared for the battle. No matter how many times I got knocked to the ground, I would get up over and over again, until I could stand strong as a proud African man and father.

But as much as I wanted to change, it would take eight years for me to have a true awakening and begin to grow into the fullness of my potential. Until then, my desire to change would do battle with the old instincts, angers, and fears I had carried into prison. True to form, chaos ensued, and for the first time during my incarceration, I would learn the true meaning of hell on earth.

PART TWO

PART TWO

11

The thought of killing myself smashed into my consciousness like a drunk driver. Images of my tattered life boiled and raged inside my mind, and a deep, piercing pain shot through my heart. It felt like someone had plunged a fiery sword through my most vital organ. I clutched my chest, struggling to reclaim control of my mind, but it was too late. I had already welcomed into my most sacred space the thought of ending it all—the pain, the fear, the sense of loneliness and abandonment.

I looked around Ralph's basement, hoping that one of my new friends would notice what was going on inside of me, but they were lost in the merriment of the forty-ounce bottles of Olde English that we had drunk that night. Instead of alerting them that something was seriously wrong, I decided to crack a joke about the pain I was feeling. With a sinister grin, I asked Ralph, Jamal, and Mike what they would do if I blew my brains all over the walls of the basement.

"Nigga, you trippin," Mike responded before taking another swig from his bottle. Ralph let out a laugh, and Jamal glanced at me for a moment before losing interest and turning to light up a cigarette.

Despite the fact that I grew up around guns and violence, suicide was something we never talked about. Back then, I didn't understand the power of depression, didn't understand how it could cause someone to end his or her life, just to get rid of the pain that person was carrying. I didn't understand that the thought of painting the walls with my brain was a cry for help, one I should take seriously. What had happened to us that allowed us to laugh away a question like that?

We continued to drink for another half an hour before Ralph decided it was time for us to wrap up the night and head home. Mike lived one block over on Murray Hill, Jamal lived two blocks over on St. Mary's, and I lived a block in the opposite direction on Ferguson. We exited through the side door of Ralph's basement, and when we reached the corner of Midland, we exchanged pounds and parted ways.

I turned and walked toward the block where I had been staying with my father and his family, my feet growing heavier with each step. It felt like the weight of the universe was on my shoulders. I was tired of searching for love and happiness. I felt unloved and unwanted at home, and I didn't fit in at my new school.

When I first moved in with my father, stepmother, stepsister, and nephew, they had shown me my makeshift bedroom in the basement with such pride. There was a bed, two reclining chairs, and a floor-model TV. I had a space I could call my own. But instead of feeling safe and warm in the space they had made for me,

I felt cold and cut off from the rest of the house. In my mind, being in the basement symbolized my standing in the family—I was a burden, and they had dealt with me by stashing me out of sight.

I decided that when I got back home, I would end it all. There was a sawed-off shotgun beneath my mattress, and I had plenty of shells. A smile crossed my face as I thought about the guilt my parents would feel when they found my bloody, headless body in the basement. Maybe then they would stop and think about what they had done when they tore our family apart. Maybe for once, my mother would feel the pain that I felt when she decided to push me out of her life and ignore me. Maybe she would cry as she remembered all of the times she told me she wished I had never been born.

I fumbled with my keys, struggling to open the side door. The house was quiet when I entered, but I knew that my stepsister Vanessa would be awake, talking on the phone. A twinge of guilt shot through me as I thought about her and my nephew Megale—how hurt and confused they would be if I went through with this. But I inhaled deeply and descended the basement stairs, stuffing those emotions down where they couldn't impede my progress toward death. I didn't bother to turn on the lights; I knew the layout of the basement like the back of my hand.

I plopped down in one of the La-Z-Boy chairs next to my bed and lit up a Newport. The calming influence of nicotine circulated throughout my body as I closed my eyes and thought about how things had been since I moved in with my father.

On the surface, everything about my setup looked good. The house sat in the middle of a pleasant, unassuming street. My stepmother's cooking was spectacular, and a genuine sibling connection had sprung up between me and my stepsister. My father and stepmother both worked for Lafayette Clinic at the time, and they gave us an allowance whenever they got paid. I had enrolled in

Cooley High School, made a few friends in the neighborhood, and had a couple of girlfriends who skipped school with me whenever the mood struck us.

But I didn't feel at home, and I wasn't happy. The longing to be loved and accepted by my mother ate at me, and the memory of her rejection made me feel unwelcome, even in the loving home my father and stepmother had managed to provide.

I knew that my father had concerns about my behavior. Prior to moving in with them, I had been arrested a few times for various crimes. I was no longer the honor roll student I had been. I rarely attended class and had lost interest in learning. I made a routine of getting kicked out of school. My father would take me back to sign me in, but as soon as he would leave, I went right out the back door.

Looking back, the most troubling thing about this part of my life is that no one ever stopped to ask me what was wrong. They never questioned how or why I had changed so dramatically in such a short span of time. Years later, during conversations with my father, I would learn about the struggles he had been facing at the time—those of being a recent divorcé and a father to three biological children and three stepchildren while trying to make a new relationship work.

As I sat there puffing on my cigarette, I thought about every beating I had suffered at the hands of my mother. I thought about the day she hurled a cast-iron pot at my head after I asked her if she wanted to see the good grade I had gotten on my test. I thought about how my brothers had never stood up for me. I thought of everything I could think of to make myself more miserable, until I had worked up the courage to reach beneath the mattress and grab the shotgun.

I held the heavy steel in my hands for a moment, then sat back down in the chair, caressing the barrel as tears began streaming from my eyes. I remembered telling my mother that I wanted to be a doctor, and more tears fell. I had told her things like that all the time—I wanted her to love me and be proud of me more than anything in the world. I couldn't summon the words to articulate why she had been wrong to abandon me, so I knew that the problem had to be with me.

I then started to think about my father and his role in the drama. I tried to make myself resent him for not being stronger as the head of the household, for not intervening when my mother beat my ass for nothing. I tried my best to make myself dislike him—to find a reason why all of this was his fault and not mine—but I couldn't. My father had his shortcomings, but he was a good man, and I could never accuse him of not loving me. I thought about how things were when it was just me and him, and more tears came. My death would break his heart, but I had to end the pain.

I checked the shotgun to ensure there was a slug in the chamber before taking off the safety. I inhaled deeply and prepared to place the barrel in my mouth, picturing the flash of pain I would feel. I wondered if the heat from the barrel would melt my lips when I pulled the trigger, wondered how much of my head would spread across the basement. I wondered how loud the gunshot would be.

This final thought stopped me cold. If I fired the shotgun, the sound would startle my nephew from his sleep. I imagined my stepsister trying to console him, and the image made me put the gun back beneath the mattress. There had to be another way.

I lit another cigarette before climbing the stairs to the top floor. As I walked through the house, I absorbed all of the details for the last time: my father's mesh air force baseball hat on the table with his house keys, lighter, and pack of Kool cigarettes. My nephew's tiny Air Jordans at the foot of the stairs.

When I reached the bathroom upstairs, I tiptoed inside and closed the door. I opened the medicine cabinet, not even bothering to turn on the light, and began eyeing the different bottles of prescription medicine inside.

I read a few of the labels with hopes that they had a warning sign on them, but I didn't find any that said something like WARNING! MAY CAUSE DROWSINESS. Once I had read each label, I began searching again, until I came across a bottle that had a lot of pills in it. It didn't have a warning sign, but I figured that if I took enough, they would do the trick.

I removed the bottle from the cabinet and opened the top, then poured out a handful of pills as I looked at myself in the mirror. My face had a ghostly appearance, and my eyes were heavy with the sadness of an orphan. I looked like I was already dead.

I took one last look at the pills in my hand, inhaled deeply, then swallowed them greedily. When the last pill snaked its way down my throat, I left the bathroom and hurried back downstairs to the kitchen, where I gulped down some water to make the pills stay down. I then slunk back down to the basement and waited for death to claim me.

All of a sudden, I was struck by the thought of how unfair it would be for me to allow my two-year-old nephew to find me dead in the basement. Each morning, I would lie in the bed and listen to the pitter-patter of his little feet as he navigated his way through the living room, dining room, and finally the kitchen, where the stairs to the basement began. He would crawl backward down the stairs, stopping periodically until his eyes had fully adjusted to the dark, and when he reached the bottom step, he would stand up, come over to my bed, and stare at me. Sometimes I would watch him through squinted eyes as he tried to assess whether I was awake. Finally, he would tap me on my face and call my name.

"Uncle Jay! Uncle Jay!" he would say as he tapped my face. "I want some cereal!" He would continue tapping me until I got up and fed him.

The thought of him coming down the next morning and not being able to wake me caused me to jump up from the chair. I was dizzy, but I made it back up the stairs and went straight to

Vanessa's bedroom. When she let me in, I sat silently on the floor beside her bed for a minute.

She asked me what was up, and I explained to her that I was trying to kill myself. I told her that I was letting her know because I didn't want Megale to find me dead in the morning. She was silent for what felt like an eternity, and when she finally spoke, I could sense the uncertainty in her voice. She asked me what I had done. I told her that I was going back to the basement to die, and she snapped into action, telling me that she was going to get my father. I begged her not to, but deep inside, I was happy that she was taking action. For the first time in years, I felt like someone cared about me.

I left Vanessa's room, walked back down to the basement, and lay across my bed. A few minutes later, I heard the heavy footsteps of my father coming down. He hit the light switch, and the bright glare from above caused me to scrunch my eyes into tight balls.

"What's wrong?" my father asked as he sat on the bed beside me. He placed his hand on my head and checked my pulse.

I told him that I didn't want to live any longer. He asked me what I had taken, and when I told him, he stood and walked upstairs. To this day, I don't know what he did up there, but when he returned, he was carrying a cup of coffee. He held my head gently and urged me to drink it. I sipped the bitter liquid as I listened to him breathe deeply.

For the next hour, he continued to talk to me as we drank coffee and smoked cigarettes. He told me how much he loved me and how smart I was. He told me that I shouldn't feel unwanted, and as much as I was hurting, I knew that he meant everything he said. When we realized that the pills I had taken were harmless and I wasn't going to die, my father sat in the La-Z-Boy chair and watched me until I fell asleep.

———

THE NEXT MORNING, nobody said a word about what had happened the night before. There were no discussions about enrolling me in counseling, no questions about why I had decided to take my life. There was no call from my mother. I knew that I wouldn't attempt to kill myself again, but I was still carrying around the pain that manifested itself in my body like a malignant tumor, and I had no idea how to cope with it.

Things spiraled downward from there. I began dabbling in the dope game again, hanging out with my older brothers in Brightmoor, a gritty neighborhood at the far west end of the city. We were selling weight and feeling like we were back in the old days, but the good times were short-lived. In the span of less than a year, I would see both of my brothers sent to prison—Alan for retaliating after someone broke into our house and stole our safe, and Art when a beef with some guys in the neighborhood escalated into violence.

By then, it had become clear that my move back home was not working out. My father and I began clashing over me staying out late at night and not going to school. Eventually, he and my stepmother separated, and so he and I moved into an apartment on Greenfield and Plymouth. But before long, I was arrested on a drug charge and sent to a Job Corps program in Prestonsburg, Kentucky.

Job Corps was an eye-opening experience. Growing up, I didn't understand much about racial dynamics. My parents had raised us to view all people as people, and since we lived in a neighborhood that was primarily white, I believed them. But during my time in Prestonsburg, I learned that bigotry still exists in some parts of the country.

Our campus sat on a plot of land surrounded by mountains and forests. We were there to better ourselves by learning trade skills and completing our educations, but there were some in the town who didn't like the fact that we were there.

One day, we were evacuated from the building because of a bomb threat. Someone had called and said they would blow up the building if our "city nigger asses" didn't leave town. It was nearly three o'clock in the morning when we were evacuated from our dorm, and we had to stand outside in the cold for what seemed like an eternity while we waited on the bomb squad to clear the building. As we stood waiting, we watched a cross burning in the woods across from the campus.

On the face of it, I was doing everything the program was designed to do. I completed my GED and learned carpentry as part of my trade requirement. But even though I was hundreds of miles from home, I had brought my old ways with me, running a black-market store and selling six-dollar joints to give myself money for clothes, alcohol, and whatever else I wanted. Then, five months into the program, I got into a fight with a security guard who had called me "boy" when he ordered me to sit down. They terminated me from the program and packed me on the next Greyhound leaving for Detroit.

As the miles rolled by on the interstate, I prepared myself for the lecture I knew I would receive from my father when I got home. He had tried his best to get me on the right path, but here I was: back in Detroit, back living the same life I had promised to leave, time and time again.

Except this time, the consequences of that life would catch up with me. And those consequences would change me forever.

12

In the months following the birth of my son, I became deeply entrenched in my anger. I felt guilty about being an absentee father, but I hadn't learned to take responsibility for the actions that led me to be taken out of my children's lives. I was learning a lot about white supremacy and the role it played in filling America's prisons with young Black males. This knowledge provided the perfect outlet for the toxic anger that was consuming me.

I anguished over each story of lynching, rape, and oppression, and I began to feel justified in my rage toward white staff and inmates. I was growing dangerously intelligent. What I didn't realize at the time was how distorted my thinking had become. Instead of going beneath the surface to the root causes of my negative thinking and violent behavior, I covered up my pain by directing it toward white people. This allowed me to justify my outbursts and remain unaccountable for my role in the mess that my life had become.

On top of that, I was broke. It didn't take much to survive financially in prison—just a few dollars here and there to buy toiletries, cigarettes, and snacks to supplement the food they served in the chow hall. But I hadn't been assigned a job yet, and none of my family and friends had sent money in time for me to make it to the store, which was only open every other week. My bunky Murder and I were running low on cigarettes, and because we didn't know when our next money orders would arrive, neither of us was in a position to borrow from other inmates.

One night, Murder and I were talking about our financial predicament and the sad fact that we couldn't even count on our so-called friends to drop a hot twenty dollars on our books. It made me think about the money my friends and I used to spend at the corner store. We would sit there all day, drinking fifths of liquor and forties of beer, smoking cigarettes and weed as we pleased. Where were those friends now that I needed them?

Murder and I continued talking, and before long, we had devised a plan to rob merchandise from our neighbor, a middle-aged white man who ran a black-market store. We talked about how our neighbor would give the brothers one store item, charge them for two items in return, and then talk down to them when they couldn't pay back what they owed him. He was no different from the other brothers on the cellblock, who would think nothing of busting another brother's head or stabbing him to death over a pack of cigarettes; but in our mind, his white skin put him in the same class as the officers who policed the prison, and we decided to rob him the next time he picked up goods for his store. The plan was for me to run into the cell and subdue him while Murder came in behind me and took his stuff.

The next day, we hung around our cell, watching our neighbor's every move and keeping an eye on the comings and goings of the officer responsible for our tier. When we noticed our neighbor's bunky heading for the shower, we knew the timing was right, so we eased back into our cell and cracked the door. I told Murder to look out for the officer while I walked by our neighbor's cell to make sure he was there.

I stepped out and walked past our neighbor's door. Out of the corner of my eye, I spotted him sitting on his bunk. I continued walking down the hall to play it off, planning to mount the attack when I returned—but when I turned around, I was shocked to see Murder halfway inside the cell, telling the guy to give up all of his store goods.

A jolt of fear shot through my body. This wasn't the plan, and it wasn't going to work. Murder's attention was split between holding up the guy and watching out for the police, and our neighbor took the opportunity to try and land a punch. Without a moment to spare, I pulled Murder out of the way and returned a blow that knocked the guy into the cell door. He staggered, covering his face, and Murder jumped on his back, choking him and trying to pull him back into the cell. What started as a robbery attempt had quickly escalated into a full-on assault; our adrenaline was pumping, and we forgot what we had come for.

I was measuring the guy up for a good punch when I felt someone jump on my back. All I could think about was his bunky sneaking up on me from behind, so I reached back and quickly leaned forward, flipping him over my back and onto the concrete floor, where he landed with a thud. It was then that I realized that this wasn't the guy's bunky; it was an officer. Before the reality of what I had done could kick in, several officers had rushed me to the wall and put me in handcuffs.

A dozen of the guards rushed to the unit, grabbing Murder and throwing him in handcuffs. As they led us away, we could hear the crackling over the radio. The officers had sent out an emergency call to the infirmary because our neighbor had begun having a seizure. The officer who had me by the cuffs told me that I would be charged with murder if the guy died en route to the hospital.

"I don't give a fuck," I snapped. "I ain't never going home anyway."

The officer ignored my bravado. He had seen it all before, and he knew that I really did care, or at least wanted to.

They brought me to the segregation unit, placing me in a shower cage with a steel door, where I stayed in handcuffs for fifteen minutes. After what felt like an eternity, an officer with the face of a hound dog came to the shower cage and ordered me to back up to the slot in the cage door where he could unlock the handcuffs. But when I backed up to the slot and held my hands up where he could reach them, he unlocked the right-hand cuff and jerked my left arm through the slot, pulling downward in a violent motion.

"So you like to assault white men, huh? You li'l asshole." The skin was tearing from my arm as he pulled down on the cuffs even harder.

"Bitch, when they let me out of the hole, I'm going to kill your hoe ass," I promised through clenched teeth, my arm bone threatening to snap against the bottom of the slot.

The officer grinned. "Next time, think twice about who you put your hands on, dickhead," he said, releasing my hand from the cuff. I wrapped my shirt around my arm to stop the flow of blood, cursing the officer and continuing to tell him what I would do to him when I got out of there.

After a moment, more officers showed up to take me to a new cell. I didn't know what they would try to do to me, so when they told me to turn around and place my hands behind my back, I hesitated and tensed up. It was then that one of the officers noticed me bleeding and asked if I wanted to see a nurse. Something about his show of concern caused me to relax, so I told him I was okay and allowed him to cuff me up.

As I was being escorted to a cell, another officer mentioned that they had rushed our neighbor to the hospital, and it wasn't looking good for us. He also asked me why I was wasting my young life. This was a question I had been asked quite often when I was young, and I never was able to give an answer. All I knew was that I was hurting inside and didn't give a fuck if I lived or died. I felt like my life was over, so there was nothing more to waste.

When I entered the cell, I sat down on the bunk and thought briefly about what my father would think when he learned that I had been charged with another count of murder. At the time, I didn't expect that I would ever get out of prison; but that didn't mean I wanted to kill another person, especially not over a bag of commissary.

I stood looking out of the window for what felt like hours before a sergeant came to my cell and read off the charges. I was given a major misconduct for assault on staff, assault on an inmate, and dangerous contraband, for a weapon they had discovered in my cell.

Within two days, Murder and I were transferred back to the Michigan Reformatory, where I would be placed on long-term segregation status.

DURING THE FORTY-MINUTE ride back to Ionia, images of the hole tumbled through my head like a gymnast. In prison vernacular, we called it "lay down." As one prisoner put it, "Because down here, all you can do is lay your ass down and read, lay your ass down and write, or lay your ass down and talk shit all day." The administration used the much more lofty euphemism "administrative segre-gation," which sounded clinical and maybe even benevolent. But when the officers weren't on record, they called it the hole just like the rest of us.

I had been in the hole before, but never for more than sixty days. I had heard the horror stories about long-term solitary: how inmates had been found hung in their cells, or mysteriously suf-focated with their own socks. I had heard how the officers would come in your cell with the goon squad and beat you two breaths short of death. More than any of the other thoughts, this one wor-ried me most. I had just injured one officer and threatened an-other. What if they had called their buddies at MR to give me a nice work-over?

After being processed in, I was escorted to a cellblock known as the "Graves." The inmates called it that because once you were thrown in the "Graves," it was as though you were dead to every-one in general population. The cells were so small that you felt like you had been squeezed into a coffin.

The first thing I noticed on entering the cellblock was the gloomy ambiance that filled the whole place. The windows were painted a somber gray, and the only natural light came from the couple of slivers that snuck through when the officers were nice enough to leave one of the windows cracked. If you wanted to know if it was morning or night, you asked an officer or guessed based on when they passed out our meals.

When I reached my cell, the bars squeaked open, and the of-ficer ordered me to step inside. Once the bars had closed, he re-moved my handcuffs and left. I looked around in disgust at the dingy cell. The bed was six inches off of the floor, and the toilet was stuffed behind a small footlocker. In order to sit down and take a dump, I had to remove my whole jumpsuit—it was the only way I could jam my legs behind the locker.

To my surprise, it was relatively quiet on the block, but I would soon learn that this was the calm before the storm. Most of the inmates in the hole slept the bulk of their days away, only waking up to get their food trays. And when the final meal of the day had been passed out, the cellblock would come alive.

When the officer made his rounds, I asked him for some cleaning supplies, but he informed me that the porters wouldn't pass them out until they came around for lunch. I continued to stand at the bars and wait—there was no way I was going to sit or lie down on a mattress that someone else had sweated and farted on.

The food portions, when they arrived, were nearly a half-size smaller than what I was used to receiving in general population. I devoured the small meal like a ravenous wolf, then placed my tray in the small slot of my cell door. I didn't really like milk, so I left the carton sitting on the locker. But when they came around to pick up trays, one of the porters whispered that I had better hide the milk in my locker unless I wanted to be placed on "food loaf." I had never heard of food loaf, the hard loaf of mashed-up food that is served to inmates as punishment.

I put the carton back on the tray, but the porter shot me another look that said, "Man, you crazy." That milk I had thrown back on the tray could have bought me a bag of cereal, some juice, or an extra piece of toast. In fact, in the hole, it was an unspoken rule that nothing was to be thrown out. If you could eat it or smoke it, it could be bartered to your advantage.

As I lay back on my bunk (which I had sanitized using supplies from the porter), my mind raced with all the thoughts I had run from in general population. I dreamt of how soft Brenda's lips used to feel against mine. I dreamt of how good it felt to guzzle down an ice-cold 40 on a hot summer day. I dreamt of the late-night laughter that echoed through the 'hood as we sat on the porch kicking it at two o'clock in the morning. My dreams were a kaleidoscope of all that my life had been, and all that I had lost.

I found myself thinking about how I had arrived at this point in my life. Growing up, I never imagined that I would end up caged in a cell, living out my life like an animal. *I'm too smart for this shit*, I thought angrily as I stared up at the paint-chipped ceiling.

At some point, all inmates begin to wonder if their existence is really a nightmare, from which at any moment they could wake up and be back home in their own beds. But as the years of your incarceration stretch on, you soon learn that prison is all too real. And for me, things were about to get more real than I could have ever imagined.

THAT NIGHT, AFTER dinner, the hum of conversation could be heard as inmates discussed religion, politics, and stories from their lives on the streets. As I sat back on my bunk, listening to guys from Flint, Saginaw, and Lansing talking about their neighborhoods, it felt like I was reliving my own memories of life before prison.

After a while, I got bored with the other inmates' conversations, so I decided to get up and write a few letters. I wrote one to Brenda, then another to my ex-girlfriend Nycci, and before I knew it, I was writing everyone I knew. The hours spun by quickly as I scratched out letter after letter with the dull tip of a two-inch pencil.

It was through these letters that I realized writing could serve as a means of escape. With a pencil and a piece of paper, it was almost like I could travel outside of prison and go wherever I desired. I could stand on the corner in my neighborhood, and no one could stop me. I could drive down the freeway to see my ex-girlfriend in Ohio, and the bars and wired fences couldn't hold me back. Writing was freedom, so I wrote till my fingers were sore.

When the lights went out at midnight, the cellblock had an

eerie feel to it. I was on the bottom floor, toward the end of the tier, and there were no lights in the hall near my cell. I climbed into my bunk and prayed that I could drift off to sleep before the memories of life on the outside came back to haunt me; otherwise, I knew that I would go insane.

As I lay there willing myself to sleep, the world around me exploded into chaos. "Get y'all bitch ass up!" a loud voice called. "Ain't no sleep around here." This was followed by a sound as loud and startling as a shotgun blast. *Boom! Boom! Boom!* The sound came relentlessly as the inmate banged down the lid of his footlocker over and over, setting into motion a chain of events that I will never forget.

For the next four hours the hole became an anarchist stronghold as inmates banged their lockers and hurled racial epithets and homophobic remarks through the air like hand grenades. Some stuffed their toilets with sheets and flushed until water cascaded over the tier like Niagara Falls. I stared out of my cell in disbelief as my floor turned into a wading pool. Trash and sheets that had been set on fire flew out of cells. The officers tried to restore order by turning off the water supply, but the mayhem continued. By the time the cellblock had begun to calm down, dawn was slowly creeping up on us.

By then, the only thing stirring in the tier was a giant rat the size of a possum, which the inmates had named "Food Loaf," after the brick of mashed-up food that was fed to disobedient inmates. I watched as Food Loaf sludged through the murky water to retrieve the soggy bread and rotted apple cores that had been thrown out onto the cellblock floors. He moved with a quiet confidence about him that came from having been around hundreds of inmates every day.

At first, I wondered why none of the inmates had killed Food Loaf. His other mousy cousins hadn't been so lucky—it's hard to live alongside vermin who climb in your bed at night or get into your footlocker and nibble on the food you have stored away. But Food Loaf was different. He was kind of like us—an outcast, and a lone survivor—and we could identify with that. So we allowed him to coexist with us.

After a few days in the Graves, I learned how to sleep through the mornings and afternoons. Meanwhile, the prison authorities were trying to determine how to punish me for my assault on the officer back at Carson City. In the midst of it all, I was transferred back to the county jail for an appeal hearing on my initial charges. Eventually, they sent me to the Maximum Security Facility at Standish, where a new level of hell awaited.

13

Detroit, Michigan
1990

"I don't care what anyone calls you," my father said as we drove away from the Greyhound bus station. "There is never an excuse to allow someone's words to stand in the way of your success." I had known he would be disappointed to learn that I had been kicked out of Job Corps, but I felt hurt by his words. I wanted him to understand why I had lashed out. I wanted him to understand how I felt being demeaned and treated inferior because of the color of my skin. I wanted him to know that I had a responsibility to myself, and those who came after me, to do something about the way we were treated in Kentucky.

What I hadn't accounted for was the fact that my father had grown up during the turbulent sixties and seventies, and had joined the military at age seventeen. He had lived through things far worse than I had, but at that point in my life, I couldn't understand why he wouldn't react in anger to the racism I had experienced.

When we got home, I basked in the familiarity of my surroundings, and within a week or so, I was back down in Brightmoor, hanging out at Tamica's house. The fellas were happy to see me, and I was happy to be back. I had missed hanging out, fighting dogs, hustling, and chasing girls with my homies. It was refreshing to be standing out on the corner again with the crew.

Things were slow for the first few weeks, but soon enough, I was able to get ahold of half an ounce of cocaine, which I cooked and cut up to sell. My boys Mack and Coop had built up a clientele on the block, but neither had a problem with me making a few dollars on the side. The reality was, no one wanted to roll all day, so we shared the business to keep the clientele from going anywhere else.

Then, one fateful night, I was lying on the couch at Tamica's when Coop tapped on the window. It was about two o'clock in the morning.

I got up and went outside to see what was up. Coop had a customer but was out of supply, so he asked if I could spare a few rocks. I went back inside the house to get my sack, which I had stashed in the freezer to ensure my nephews didn't get to it. When I came back out, I gave a bag to Coop and told him to come back and tap on the window when he had made the transaction.

Five minutes later, I was on the couch, drifting back to sleep, when I heard the faint sound of someone screaming my name. For a minute, I thought I was dreaming, but then the sound grew louder. I jumped up from the couch and swung open the front door to see what was going on. When I looked outside, I didn't see anyone in front of the house—but just as I was about to turn and go back in, I heard Coop's baby's mother calling my name out of a window across the street. The first thing that crossed my mind was that Coop was about to beat her up (even though I had never seen him abuse her). But before I could make sense of what was going on, Coop burst through his mother's front door holding a .357 Magnum in his hand.

"This bitch tried to rob me! This bitch tried to rob me!" he shouted as I walked over to the house. My initial thought was that a woman, possibly his baby's mother, had tried to hold him up. This wasn't uncommon in our line of work. The streets were cutthroat, and anyone involved in the lifestyle was capable of any level of disloyalty, betrayal, and treachery.

Coop went back inside his mother's house, and I climbed the porch steps of the house slowly, trying to process what was going on. Was Coop trying to pull off a cover-up to justify not having my money? I didn't know what to think as I entered the house, but when I stepped over the threshold, there was a man lying on the living room floor. He was dressed in dark pants and a dark sweater that was saturated with blood.

"Please, I'm dying," he said. His breaths were labored, and the sound of gurgling blood was coming from his chest.

"I'm about to shoot this bitch in the head!" Coop screamed, standing over the dying man. "He was going to kill my whole family. My mama, my sisters, and my baby is in here."

It took me a few minutes to calm Coop down to the point where he could explain what had happened. Earlier that day, the man had come by to buy some rocks, and he returned later with the .357 and a pocket full of ammo. Coop let him in and came to get the rocks he had borrowed from me, but on his return, the man pulled the gun on him and told him to get on his knees. He removed a bullet from his pocket and told Coop to bite it, to prove that it was real. He told Coop that he wasn't playing, that he would kill everyone in the house unless Coop showed him where the rest of the dope was. As Coop sat on his knees staring down the barrel of the .357, all he could think about was his daughter, mother, sister, and daughter's mother. It was these thoughts that gave him the courage to fight back.

In a burst of adrenaline, Coop rushed the man, lifted him up, and slammed him onto the kitchen floor. The force of the blow dislodged the gun from the man's hand, and in one motion, Coop scrambled, picked up the gun, and fired it into the man's chest.

I told Coop to have his mother call the police and report the robbery attempt—that it would keep him from being charged with anything. But Coop's judgment had been clouded. He said that he wanted to take the body across the street and dump it in the backyard of the vacant house next to Tamica's. I tried to talk him out of it, but he was determined to get the body out of his mother's house. At the time, I didn't have the courage to stand up and make him do the right thing—all I could do was be a friend in the only way I knew how.

As we stood in the vacant yard across the street, staring down at the man, I don't remember feeling anything. I didn't care that the man was lying dead. I rationalized my way out of it by saying that it could have easily been Coop and his family. Looking back, it sickens me to think that at such a young and fragile age, I had already developed a callousness that would prevent me from having compassion and empathy for someone who had been killed.

I was lost in thought when, out of nowhere, Coop fired several more shots into the man's body. To this day, I think those shots were a cover for what Coop really wanted to do, which was cry. His family had been threatened, and he had been made to bite the bullet that was meant to kill him. No man wants to live knowing his actions could've brought devastation on his family.

Coop told me to have Tamica call the police in the morning and tell them the dog had found a body in the backyard next door. The next morning, when the police arrived to investigate, Coop came and joined us in the backyard. The detectives had only been investigating the scene for a few minutes when they found a trail of blood that led back to Coop's mother's house. They questioned Ms. Cooper and arrested Mack, thinking he was Coop. The detectives said no charges would have been filed had the body not been removed from the house.

Coop eventually turned himself in and was sentenced to five years in prison. Before he left, Coop vouched for me with his brother Boe, who was running a drug operation of his own. Coop told Boe that if he could trust anyone to do good work for him, it was me.

Boe brought me on board on an exclusive basis, and we quickly bonded. By that spring, the warm weather was bringing more and more people out onto the street, and our clientele was growing by the day. We would stay on the porch from sunup to sundown, selling drugs and drinking. Even though we were bringing illegal activity to the street, most of our neighbors loved us, especially the girls, and it felt like our block was becoming the heart of the neighborhood. Everyone wanted to be down with the guys from Blackstone.

But on March 8, 1990, the good times—and the last remnants of my childhood—were shattered by a burst of gunfire.

TWENTY-FIVE YEARS LATER, I can still remember where I was standing when the gunman drove by. I remember what I was wearing, whom I was with, and where we were headed. More than anything, I remember the intense heat that raged through my body when the first bullet met its mark.

It all started with an argument over a girl. The previous summer, before I caught the case that sent me to Job Corps, I had been dating an older woman named Angie. Angie had promised to come and spend time with me once I got home, but when that day finally came, she stood me up. I felt betrayed, so when I ran into her the next day at the store, I told her how I felt. She apologized, but then told me the reason she hadn't come to see me: She had started seeing someone while I was away. I couldn't believe it, and I lashed out.

"Why the fuck you couldn't just be real about it?" I vented. "You lied to me over and over again through letters, and now you telling me this bullshit. Fuck you, you stupid-ass lying bitch."

Little did I know how much those words would cost me.

Two days later, a car pulled up to the corner where I was standing talking to Boe. When I looked up and saw Angie's new boyfriend in the driver's seat, I knew it was going to be trouble.

"What the fuck you say to my woman the other day at the store?" he said forcefully.

"Fuck that bitch and fuck you!" I said, not willing to be intimidated.

These were fighting words. In an environment where the line between disrespect and danger is razor-thin, calling a man's woman a bitch gives him no choice but to defend her honor and his reputation.

"What up, get your punk ass out of the car!" I shouted, inviting the fight that I already knew was coming. But I had no clue what he would choose to fight *with*.

A smirk crossed his face as he reached down and pulled out a pistol.

I was unarmed, and before I could turn and run for shelter, he squeezed off several shots, hitting me twice in the leg and once in the foot.

When the first of the three bullets tore into my flesh, I felt my shinbone crack. Immediately, my shoe filled with blood, sloshing around as I fled the scene, trying to escape my assailant. I zigzagged back and forth, dodging the fusillade of bullets and praying that none of them would hit me in my spine—or worse, the back of my head. (One bullet remains lodged in my foot to this day, a reminder of how fragile life can be in the 'hood.)

I ran around the corner and into the house of a young lady named Lisa, who had witnessed the whole incident. As I approached her, she begged me not to come in, but I ran right past her and through her front door. I sat there trying to gather myself, my emotions boiling and raging like a violent storm at sea. My initial fear was replaced by a deep feeling of loneliness, and then anger. I couldn't comprehend why someone would attempt to kill me over a meaningless argument.

When I came back out, Tamica sprinted down the block and embraced me. She hadn't known if I was still alive. We walked back to her house, where I took off my jacket and shirt to check for bullet wounds. I was sweating profusely, and my mouth was so dry it felt as though someone had stuffed a handful of sand in it. I pulled out a pack of Newports, but before I could light one up, I jumped up to go inside and get a gun. I wanted to shoot someone so bad, it was killing me. I hated being a victim, and the only thing that would restore balance was getting revenge.

Tamica and Ms. Cooper did their part to calm me down. I lit up a crumpled Newport and sat on the porch, sulking as I waited for an ambulance that never showed up. This wasn't a surprise; we were used to calling 911 and never having anyone come to our rescue. After waiting close to half an hour, Boe drove me to Mount Carmel Hospital. On the way, he reassured me that everything would be all right.

When we arrived at the hospital, I felt like I was being moved through an assembly line manned by robots. The staff didn't show me any extra compassion—in Detroit, it was business as usual to see a child who had been shot. Their mouths were as taut as a tightrope as they glanced at me stoically. Before rushing me off to the X-ray room, they gave me a shot of Demerol, which knocked me out for the next couple of hours.

When I awoke, the room was full of police officers. Their demeanor was callous and confrontational as they asked me a barrage of questions about the shooter. I told them that I didn't know who shot me. (Even in my sorry state, there was a code that said you don't snitch to the police no matter what. I had never violated it before, and there was no way I was going to violate it now.)

The officers could tell I was lying, and it angered one of them to the point where he said, "That's why your li'l Black ass is lying in the bed suffering from a gunshot wound." He hurled a few more invectives at me before exiting the room. "Y'all li'l dumb-ass niggas think y'all tough until you find your stupid asses in the hospital." I felt victimized all over again, this time by an officer who didn't seem to give a damn about my misfortune.

When the doctor arrived, I felt a sense of relief, thinking that with him I could let down my guard and express my fears like the child that I was. But I was quickly reminded that we live in a cold and indifferent world. The doctor looked at my chart and left without saying much to me, returning moments later with a pair of needle-nose pliers. He dug the pliers into my flesh and wrenched the bullet from my leg, pulling bits of meat and bone with it. He irrigated it, then left to write a prescription for some antibiotics. I dozed back off under the influence of more painkillers and was awakened later by my father, stepmother, and mother.

My father's eyes were full of hopelessness, and I could see that my mother was paralyzed by fear. They were clearly at a loss for words. After all, what could they have said to me? There aren't any parenting manuals that explain how to handle your child getting shot in the streets like a rabid dog. So we talked briefly about me coming home and leaving the street life alone—a plan that we all knew wouldn't happen—then they all left.

Throughout the whole ordeal, no one hugged me. No one had counseled me or told me that everything would be okay. No one came to talk to me and explain all of the emotions I was feeling. No one told me that if I didn't find a way to deal with the fear I felt, I would become paranoid; would reach a point where I would rather victimize someone else than become a victim. No one explained to me that cars weren't galloping chariots of death, driven by the grim reaper himself.

So I coped in the only way I knew how. I became angry, and for the first time in my life, I began carrying a gun with me everywhere I went. Fourteen months later, I would be the one pulling the trigger.

14

STANDISH MAXIMUM CORRECTIONAL FACILITY
Standish, Michigan
1992

It was a sunny, warm fall day when I arrived at the Standish Maximum Security Facility. I was a year into my prison sentence and a few months past my twentieth birthday.

Despite the nice weather on my day of arrival, I soon learned that there was nothing warm or pleasant about maximum security. Our movement was heavily restricted, and we were basically locked down all day, even in general population. The officers had complete control, and they did everything they could to strip us of the few privileges we had. They enforced the rules to the letter, and any infraction was met with harsh punishment.

In the intake room, I maintained a stoic expression as the officers talked their tough correctional officer talk.

"Inmate 219184, welcome to Standish Max," a burly officer

said. "You are now in the major leagues, so think twice before you try any of the cute shit you pulled at Carson City. We don't play that shit here, you understand?" By now, I was more than used to the psychological warfare that the officers waged against the inmates, so I ignored him and focused my thoughts on how I was going to get out of solitary.

As I glanced around the room, an officer began removing the black box that had been wrapped around my handcuffs to prevent an escape. Once the box had been removed, a different officer approached with a pair of handcuffs that were attached to what looked like a dog leash. This was the first time I had seen anything like it, and my immediate thought was that this had to be a violation of the Universal Declaration of Human Rights. But I guess in the prisoncrat's mind, being leashed like a dog didn't violate Article 5 of the Declaration, which states that no one shall be subjected to "degrading treatment or punishment."

An officer placed the new handcuffs on me as one of his colleagues removed the first pair, working in tandem to minimize the time in which either of my hands was free. After removing one pair of shackles and replacing them with another, the officers chatted with each other until it was time for the transfer officers to leave. They then took me to the hole in Cellblock 1, holding tightly to my leash as I shuffled down the hall.

The layout of this prison was completely different from the Reformatory. Inside the unit were four wings—two upper and two lower. I was taken to the lower wing. The first thing I noticed was that the hallways were free of debris, and instead of cell bars, there were large steel doors with window covers on them. We reached the cell that would be mine, and the door slid open. When I stepped inside on the officers' orders, the door slid shut behind me. An officer removed my handcuffs and shackles through the food slot, and as he was preparing to leave, I asked him if my window shutter could remain open. He said no, then banged it shut.

For the first time in my short incarceration, I felt truly alone. It was a spartan cell. A flat green mattress lay folded on top of a thick slab of concrete that protruded from the side wall. On the back wall, there was a shorter slab of protruding concrete, which I soon discovered was the writing surface (or television stand, for those who had a TV). A steel toilet-sink combination sat in the corner by the door, and a large metal locker was bolted to the floor next to the concrete bed.

I sat back on my bed, and a few minutes later, a piece of thick paper came sliding beneath my door, attached to a string. I didn't know what it was, so I just sat on my bunk staring down at it until someone called out my cell number and told me to pull on the line. I had no idea what was happening, so I came to the door and asked who it was. Turns out, it was my neighbor across the hall.

I climbed down on the floor, peeked under the door, and saw that the string was coming from the cell in front of mine. As I began pulling, I noticed a few magazines slide from beneath his door. Stuffed between the magazines was a short note in which my neighbor introduced himself and let me know that if I ever needed something else to read, I could just holler over at him. His name was Lowrider. He was an older guy, and seemed quiet and laid back, but a couple of days later, I learned that he was in the hole for having sliced up the face of an inmate who owed him some money and failed to pay on time. It was proof that even the most mild-mannered of men could be pushed to aggression in order to survive the rigors of prison life. Still, Lowrider was a cool dude, and I appreciated how on my first day at Standish, he had gone out of his way to make my life a little easier.

Within a couple of days, I had gotten into a nice routine. Standish had a well-stocked library, so I started sending over for books whenever I could. I read a few novels by Stephen King and discovered how creative an author's imagination could be. It was also during this stretch that I read *Roots* for the first time and got hip to Terry McMillan. Reading was my refuge, and whenever it came time for the library to drop off our library books, I felt like Santa Claus had just come sliding down the chimney.

It was also during this time that I became acquainted with the psychological disorders that plague so many inmates. In the early nineties, a series of budget cuts had forced the state to close down a number of its mental health institutions, and this trend continued throughout the decade, during which time the patients from defunct clinics were herded into various state prisons. Patients with psychiatric needs are difficult to manage in general population, so most of them end up being housed in administrative segregation, where the hostile environment of the hole exacerbates their psychiatric problems.

One day at Standish, they moved an inmate named Reed across the hall from me. As they were putting him in the cell, he and the officers had a heated exchange. Once the officers had gotten Reed inside, I heard them ordering him to turn around so that they could remove the mask from his face. Peering out the crack beneath my door, I caught a glimpse of the officers carrying a black mesh mask that looked to be straight out of a fetish magazine. I would later learn that they placed these masks on inmates who were considered spitters or biters.

When lunchtime rolled around, the officers returned to Reed's cell and asked him if he wanted his food loaf. He told them to get the hell away from his door; he'd rather starve to death. I looked down at the small rations on my tray, and hungry as I was, I knew I couldn't eat without offering to share some with Reed. I liked that he wasn't willing to bow down and accept inferior treatment.

I slid my "car"—paper that we folded and attached to a string in order to communicate with our neighbors—over to Reed's cell with a small note attached to ask if he wanted half of my food. He wrote back that he did. I divided half my food and put it in several envelopes, and slid them across to him on my line. He pulled in the package quickly to avoid being detected by the officers.

For the next two weeks, I shared every meal with Reed, until he finally got off of meal restriction.

When they passed out our trays that day, Reed called me to the door. Sometimes on first shift, when one of the cool officers was working, they would leave our window shutters open until they picked up trays, or until they got ready to change shifts. This was the first time they had left Reed's window open, so this was my first chance to see him face-to-face. He was a tall, corpulent brother with a full beard that made him look like a brown-skinned version of the Ayatollah Khomeini.

"What's going on, Reed?" I asked as I approached the door.

"You know what?" he began.

"Naw, what?" I asked.

"Man, you a bitch-ass dick sucker. Now, get your hoe ass on your bunk and lay down," he said, breaking up into a maniacal laughter.

I stood there with my mouth agape and my temper burning as Reed continued to hurl insult after insult at me. This was the first time I had been blatantly disrespected in prison, and I was completely thrown off. Add to this the fact that I had shared half of my meal with this man for two weeks, starving myself and risking being caught and placed on food loaf along with him. I made up my mind that once I was released from the hole, I was going to stab Reed in the neck the very first chance I got. I had to; otherwise the rest of the inmates would feel like they could get away with disrespecting me, or worse.

When I was released to general population a few weeks later, I waited patiently for the day that Reed would get out and I would get my shot at him. But the day never came. As I would learn over the years, there were some inmates who did their entire sentence in the hole to prevent other inmates from getting to them. Any-time these inmates were scheduled for release, they would go out of their way to catch another misconduct, forcing the Security Classification Committee to keep them locked away.

BY THE TIME I hit the yard again, I had been in solitary confine-ment for nearly a year. It felt strange, walking from the segrega-tion unit back to the regular blocks, and it took a minute for me to adjust to walking without shackles and handcuffs.

As I approached my new unit, a group of inmates was released for chow. I walked slowly through the crowd, trying to find a fa-miliar face, but there were none to be found. Most of the guys were in their thirties and forties, which made me feel out of place. Their faces were hopeless, creased with the bitter, jagged lines of stress that mark men doing time in prison.

I was assigned a cell and informed that our unit had already been to chow and yard, so I wouldn't be able to leave my cell again until the following morning for breakfast. I didn't own a radio, tape player, or television like the other inmates around me, so I pulled out the Bible and began reading it. When I tired of that, I picked up the Quran and read a few surahs, then said a prayer and sat back on my bunk, listening to the chatter around me. A few in-mates stood at their doors talking to one another about what was on television, and I began to feel sad and left out. Up to that point in my bit, I hadn't received much financial support from my family or friends, and it hurt. Televisions cost around eighty-nine dollars, and I didn't have a quarter in my account.

When that thought hit me, it nearly caused me to break down. I began cursing everyone who had ever said they loved me. I felt like it was me against the world. My anger began to boil and rage, and I started doing push-ups to release some of the pain and frustration. I don't remember how many I did in the first set, but I do remember how I refused to get up until my muscles were burning and so tight that I thought they would pop.

On the yard the next day, I met up with a guy I had known on the outside named Day Day. When Day Day found out I had just been released from the hole, he sent me some candy bars and bags of chips, and told me to let him know if I ever needed anything. He also introduced me to a few Melanic brothers who were in our unit. I had officially joined the organization back at Carson City, but I was having trouble feeling at home in it. The brothers I had met were cool, but like the inmates I had seen on the way to my block, they were older, and we didn't have much in common.

For the first couple of weeks, I kept mostly to myself. Every morning, I would do push-ups in my cell before taking a shower and spending the rest of the day reading until the wee hours of the morning. When they turned the lights out, I would stand by my door, reading by the sliver of light that crept through the window.

After a couple of weeks, I started hooping with Day Day and a few other guys in the unit, and they invited me to join their basketball team. The basketball court was one of the proving grounds on the yard. The games were competitive and the tempers ran hot, so if you stepped onto the court, you had better be ready to defend yourself, in every sense of the word. "No blood, no foul" was the rule, and with the amount of trash talking that went on, it was common for inmates to play basketball with a shank in the sole of their shoe. A hard foul could lead to a stabbing or, worse, a riot.

Winning meant everything to us. We had been told we were losers our entire lives, and none of us wanted to have that confirmed in anything that we did. In reality, these were meaningless games designed to keep us distracted from our situation, but we took losing personally, as if it defined who we were. Despite the fact that basketball was a constant source of conflict, stabbings, and even murder, the courts stayed full, and the libraries stayed empty.

The first conflict I was involved in at Standish came when KO, one of my Melanic brothers, cursed out a brother name Rimmer-Bey, who was officiating the game. Rimmer-Bey was a respected member of the Moorish Science Temple of America, a group also known as the Moabites. The gym became tense when KO refused to back down from his insults, and one of Rimmer-Bey's cronies came over, acting like he was going to fight.

We were firm believers that you should always come to the aid of a worthy brother, so I stepped up, ready to jump in the fray. The fight never came, but I would learn later that the guy who had come to Rimmer-Bey's defense had been a hit man back in Jackson. The guys marveled at how I stood up to him, and it added to my credibility on the yard.

When the basketball season concluded, I vowed not to participate next time, because I realized that KO was a hothead serving a life sentence, and the basketball court was where he took out his frustration. I had just gotten out of solitary, and I wasn't trying to go back over a basketball game.

AFTER ABOUT A MONTH, I was transferred to another unit. I was fortunate to be put in a cell there near a few cool guys who would sneak me their radios and tape players whenever they could, letting me use them for a couple of days at a time. Some other brothers in the unit would send me books by J. A. Rogers, Ivan Van Sertima, Marcus Garvey, and Dr. Chancellor Williams. With each book that they fed me, I felt a part of my soul growing and opening up to commune with my ancestors. I immersed myself in African history and imagined what it was like in ancient Kemet (which had been renamed Egypt by the Greeks). I thought about the pyramids, which have stood the test of time, and wondered how they had been engineered. I thought about Timbuktu and how that society had created a vast trove of knowledge that was the envy of the world. In the short time I was at Standish, I learned more about African history than I had ever learned during all of my years in school.

One day on the yard, I heard a lot of buzz among the brothers. They were excited because a Melanic named Baruti was being moved into our unit. Baruti had a head full of long locks that flowed down his back, and he was ripped with lean muscle from his routine of running several miles a day. The brothers held Baruti in high esteem for his discipline and integrity. He was being moved there after serving time in Ionia Super Max; he had been charged with having caused the death of another inmate. If you believed what the brothers were saying, Baruti had been charged on flimsy evidence and shady testimony. But I always took this kind of information with a grain of salt.

When I finally met Baruti, I was impressed with his calm, quiet demeanor. He wasn't boastful about his exploits in prison. Instead, he was a wise teacher who taught mostly through his actions. Every morning when we hit the yard, he would focus on his exercise, running vigorously to outpace and outdistance everyone out there. On the days we held study group to discuss what we were reading and what was happening in the world, he always gave me encouraging words. He told me never to take anything at face value and to always be diligent in my research. When I made valid points to help build up the brothers, he would give me a nod and tell me to continue.

Baruti began treating me as if he were an uncle or an older brother, and our relationship made me proud to be a Melanic. He invited me to work out at the pull-up bars with him and a brother named Tim Gree-Bey. At first, the other guys laughed at me; even though I had an athletic build and could do push-ups all day, I could only manage one or two pull-ups before my arms started shaking with exhaustion. But Baruti and Tim told me to never give up, and within a couple of weeks, I went from doing one or two reps a set to doing ten to fifteen.

I continued to absorb as much wisdom as I could during the study sessions with the older brothers. We called these sessions "building," because their point was to help us construct new lives for ourselves based on spiritual and cultural principles of reciprocity, love, and compassion. "No matter what you do while you are in here," Baruti would tell me, "never give up on learning and trying to be a better person." I didn't always listen to him, but over the years, I would find all that he shared with me to be of great value.

I will never forget how the brothers in the library embraced me when they saw that I came consistently to check out books. Whenever a new title arrived by a Black author, they would hold it for me, and eventually it got to the point where anytime I showed up, they would already have books picked out for me. The brothers made me give detailed reports on the books they gave me, in part because they wanted to know whether they were worth reading, but also because they wanted to make sure I had read them myself. It was because of the wise counsel of Baruti and the other brothers, and the way they challenged me to think, that I was able to leave prison with a sense of purpose.

BUT THIS DIDN'T mean that everything I learned or did in the Melanics was positive. This was still prison, still a place ruled by the law of the jungle. And it was through our organization that I became even more practiced in the art of calculated violence.

One day on the yard, I was informed that we were having a security meeting. These informal meetings were organized by the members who were responsible for protecting the brotherhood. Earlier that day, an inmate in another cellblock had gotten into an altercation with one of our members, and it ended with him kicking the brother's store goods all over the yard. On its own, this might seem like a petty incident, but it wasn't something we could overlook. If we didn't retaliate, it could expose us to a more serious attack by other organizations.

During our security meeting, we discovered that the inmate who was responsible for the attack would be working on the yard crew when we were let out for recreation the next day. We began planning our retaliation, and the head of security asked if I wanted to help execute the mission. I agreed without hesitation. I was tired of seeing the other organizations watching us, waiting to see if we would do anything about the incident. Another brother, who was built like an all-pro NFL safety, said he would ride with me, so we strategized with the security staff to set the play in motion the following day. The tricky part would be finding a way to do it without being caught by the officers or the security cameras.

When we settled on a plan, I went back to my regular routine of working out and talking to Tim and Baruti. I wasn't allowed to discuss the security meeting, but I could tell that the two of them knew what was going on. As we continued working out, Baruti stopped me and said something that it would take a few years for me to appreciate. He told me that I should never allow anyone to misuse me, including my comrades.

At the time, I didn't fully understand what he was trying to say, but over the years, it would come to make sense. Baruti could see the loyalty I had for my brothers and our cause, but he also saw the naïveté that was common among young, impressionable inmates like me. We held a quixotic view of the movement, and our loyalty was often misguided—something the older, wiser members many times took advantage of. Baruti knew he couldn't tell me not to go through with the play, but as I reflect on that day, I know that's what he wished he could say.

When we arrived on the yard the next day, it was time to set our play in motion. The tension in the air was thick. We had alerted the other organizations that we were going to retaliate, and they were all waiting to see when it would happen. For the first time I could remember in my time at Standish, the basketball court was empty.

I could feel my hands sweating as I walked across the yard to meet at the security council's regular spot. We greeted one another, and after a quick briefing, one of the brothers produced a crudely sharpened piece of steel with torn bedsheets wrapped around the bottom as a handle. He passed me the shank, and it looked menacing sitting in my hand. The brother who had agreed to ride with me produced a shank of his own, and we went over the plan for one last time before leaving the meeting post.

We left our spot and walked a few laps around the track, waiting for our prey to reach a location where we knew the cameras wouldn't be able to see us. As many cameras and gun towers as the prisons had, there were always blind spots, and every inmate knew they were death traps. But our target was clueless as to what was about to happen, and it didn't take long for him to begin moving in the direction we desired. As he approached the camera's blind spot, we quickened our pace, sneaking up behind him. Before he could put together what was happening, it was too late.

I grabbed him by his shirt and stabbed him several times in the back and side. When the shank first pierced his skin, he hollered out "What I do?" We stabbed him a few more times before he took off running across the yard.

We then turned and walked toward the far end of the track, where the other security members were waiting to retrieve the shanks. Once the weapons were secured, we took off jogging on the track, blending in with the rest of the joggers, and by the time we reached the pull-up bars, the officers were administering first aid to our target. Within minutes, a siren sounded, and the guards ordered all of us in the yard to go back to our units.

The following day, the yard was abuzz over the stabbing, and our reputation was restored. It was the law of the jungle, and we had acquitted ourselves in full. But even as I basked in the praise of my brothers and the fear of the other inmates, I was feeling conflicted. On one hand, here I was learning about our history and culture and reading about how we needed to love and care for our brothers. On the other hand, whenever a brother did something that we felt violated our code of honor, we dealt with it by stabbing him or busting him in the head. It was a contradiction that never sat well with me, and it wouldn't be long before it challenged me to make some tough decisions about the Melanics and my role in the organization.

THE REST OF my yearlong stay at Standish was uneventful, and it wasn't long before I was transferred back to the Michigan Reformatory. When I told Baruti where I was going, his eyes lit up with excitement. He told me that his son was there and asked that I connect with him. Little did I know, Baruti and I would be forever connected, even though we wouldn't see each other again for another sixteen years.

My third stint at MR, beginning in 1992, was the most important leg of my journey through the belly of the beast. In the midst of daily stabbings, human despair, and overt racism, the man Shaka was born and the boy Jay was laid to rest. It was during this stretch that I would come to acknowledge things my father had been trying to teach me for years—that I was intelligent, that I possessed leadership qualities that could be used for good or bad, and that the choice was up to me. It was there at the Reformatory that I began to understand the power of empathy and human compassion.

But my transformation didn't happen overnight. First, I would have to sink lower as I fought to overcome the violent legacy of my past.

MY FIRST MONTH back at the Reformatory was an adjustment period. I knew I would be there for a while and had to figure out how to make the best of my time. I settled in with a new group of Melanic brothers and met Baruti's son, Yusef. I was excited to meet a young lion who had the same kind of fire that I had. Both of us were veterans of the streets, and trust was something that didn't come easy, so it took a couple of weeks for us to feel each other out. But we soon began building a bond based on our love of reading and our desire to make a difference in the world.

I also started having deep discussions with brothers from other organizations. At Standish, we brothers from different organizations had kept to ourselves, but back at the Reformatory, I began reaching out to other crews because I felt that it was important to find common ground with the fifteen hundred young men who were sharing our space. We held different philosophical and theological views, but we had all come from the same hopeless backgrounds, and we were all caught in the gears of the same heartless machine. Because of my willingness to learn and understand the teachings of the other organizations, I was able to build solid allegiances and bring an end to some of the violence that was standard between groups.

One day, when I was returning from my work detail, an officer called out over the PA to let me know that I had a visit. By that time, Brenda and I had decided to end our relationship, and she was struggling taking care of our son, Li'l Jay, so my father and stepmother had let her leave him with them while Brenda worked on getting her life back on track. I had never gotten a visit in my previous two stays at the Michigan Reformatory, and I didn't know what to expect, so I showered and rushed back to my cell to dress in some clothes I had borrowed from one of the brothers. (I didn't have my own clothes yet, and I sure didn't want to go for a visit in my state blues.)

When I entered the visiting room, I was directed upstairs, where my father and two younger sisters were sitting with Li'l Jay. My heart began pounding like an African drum as I studied my two-year-old son from head to toe. The sight of his little fat cheeks melted my prison toughness like butter on hot toast. I greeted my father and sisters with a hug and smile, then attempted to pick up my son. But as I drew close to Li'l Jay, he shrank back in fear.

I wanted to die on the spot. It took all of the energy I had to hold back from bursting into tears. But my father intervened with words of wisdom.

"It's okay," he reassured me. "He'll come to you. It just takes him a little bit of time to warm up to people."

My father had a point, but in my head I was screaming, *I'm not people, I'm his father!* I remained silent, however, and took a seat with my family.

We talked about what was going on back home, and it made me want to find a way to break out of prison that very day. After a half hour of talking, Li'l Jay finally became comfortable enough with me to allow me to pick him up. I held him close to me so that he could feel my heartbeat and the undeniable love that I had for him. He smiled and laughed, and for the short time that I held him, he erased the prison walls that held me captive. I could see my own and Brenda's features in him. He was a beautiful baby, and I wanted nothing more than to protect him from the cruel, ugly world that he had been born into.

After about an hour and a half, Li'l Jay started to fuss and get cranky, and my father said that it was time to leave and let him take a nap. I hugged Li'l Jay tightly, one last time, before handing him over to my father. I then notified the officers that my family was ready to go.

We were escorted downstairs, and when I exited the visiting room, I turned around to see my family standing on the other side of the bars. I smiled and waved, and Li'l Jay lifted his arms up like he wanted me to pick him up. In that moment, every fiber in my body wanted to rip through the bars to get to my son.

"Mr. White, it's time for you to return to your cell," the officer said, jarring me from my thoughts. I turned and looked at the officer with a burning anger, and he lowered his head as he led me into the strip-search room. I felt numb as I removed my clothes for the search. All I could think about was the look of disappointment that crossed Li'l Jay's face when he realized that I wasn't able to leave with him.

I HAD BEEN trying to settle down into a groove and focus on doing my time, but that visit changed me. The thought of how vulnerable my son was without me there to guide and protect him made me unable to handle the idea of remaining in prison. Mentally, I rebelled, sinking deeper into anger and depression, and this manifested in my actions toward the staff and other inmates.

No matter how much time I spent building with the brothers, I was always on edge. I developed a serious "wish a motherfucker would" attitude, hoping that someone would get out of line so that

I could release my pain by inflicting harm on him. A week after the visit from my family, I was presented with the opportunity.

Back at Carson City, an inmate had accused me of stealing his vending machine card. It was a false accusation, and the officers found out as much in their investigation, but it never stopped me from wanting to get revenge on the guy. Now that same inmate had transferred into MR.

One day, my chance at revenge came when our unit was assigned a substitute officer who wasn't as alert as the one who normally patrolled our block. When they broke our cells for chow and the target of my revenge walked down the tier, I approached him swiftly while my neighbor positioned himself in front of us, blocking the officer's view.

I seized him by the neck. "I told you I was going to get your rat ass," I said, pushing his head through a nearby window and shattering the glass with his face.

It felt good, and I never got caught. But while the brief adrenaline rush soothed my pain for the afternoon, it had faded by the next day. I needed to hurt someone else, and I did.

A week later, I choked a fellow inmate over an unpaid debt and beat up another guy over a bad call on the basketball court. It was as though I were an emotional vampire, forced to drain blood from unsuspecting victims in order to keep myself alive. I got away with most of my assaults, but I was quickly earning a reputation as an extremist. And the following month, I was sent to solitary confinement for throwing a dangerously hot tray of mashed potatoes in the face of an inmate who had insulted me.

When I reached the hole, I paced back and forth in my cell like a caged beast, raging at the other inmate for having snitched on me. The calluses on my heart and mind were thickening, and my soul had become infected with the worst and deadliest of all illnesses: self-hate. I was disappointed that I had allowed my anger to get the best of me. I was even more disappointed that I had resorted to assaulting another young Black male. My actions stood in stark contrast to the man I said I was trying to become. I desired to be a strong Black man and a leader, but my actions showed that I was still little more than a street thug.

15

Released from the hospital, I returned to my block a deadlier person than the man who had shot me. For the next fourteen months, anger would become my mask and shield as I navigated my way through the streets. The last remaining shreds of my innocence had been killed, but at the time, I was blind to what was happening on the inside.

I became obsessed with carrying a gun, treating my 9-millimeter Taurus like a crackhead treats his pipe. I went to bed with my gun, woke up with it, and wouldn't so much as take a dump without it being in arm's reach. At the first sign of a confrontation, I was ready to shoot.

During this time, I was traveling back and forth from Ohio, selling crack there for two to three times the amount we sold it for in Detroit. It was a lucrative venture, and it provided us great opportunities to buy more guns—which we needed because the local dealers didn't like the fact we were making more money than they were. As the violence between us and them intensified, we realized that we couldn't win a protracted war on the other dealers' terrain, so we closed up shop and headed home.

I returned to Detroit ready to pick up where I left off, but things had cooled down on the block. If I wanted to make any money, I knew I had to figure out a way to turn the heat back up on Blackstone.

I reached out to some of our old customers to tell them we were going to start selling again, and slowly but surely they started coming back. Things were still slow, but I was making enough money to stay fresh and take care of basic necessities. It didn't compare to the money I had been raking in before, but I had faith that Blackstone would rebound and the money would soon come rolling in.

I had been back for a week when I took notice of the new neighbors who had moved into the house next door to Tamica. They were a family, and although I didn't know any of them, it wasn't long before I noticed that a bunch of young ladies were going in and out of the house. From all appearances, it was mostly females living there, and that was right up my alley. Our crew had built a reputation for hooking up with all the females in the neighborhood, and I knew it wouldn't be long before I made good on that reputation with the girls next door.

A week or so later, I noticed that a few of our old customers were stopping through the house next door, which made me wonder if someone over there was selling dope. My thoughts were confirmed when one of our old customers stopped by our crib and asked me if that was our operation.

Later that same day, one of the girls who lived in the house came outside and approached me. She was light-skinned with a pretty smile and silky, jet-black hair. She was dressed in a sweat suit with her hair pulled back in a ponytail. As she approached the porch, I laughed inside at how confident she appeared to be.

When she got there, she asked, "Do you have a pistol I can borrow?" Her voice sounded casual and relaxed, as if she were asking to borrow a cup of sugar.

At first, I wondered why on earth a girl like that would need a gun—and if she did, why she was approaching a complete stranger for it. Then I thought about the activity next door and some of the things I had seen over the years selling dope, and my thoughts turned to a small .25-caliber Raven I had purchased from one of our customers. I told the girl that she could use it, but she had to return it.

I didn't think about the fact that I was a teenager giving another teenager a gun. All I could think was, if I ever had needed a pistol from her, I would've wanted her to give it to me without asking.

Later that night, she came back to the house, and I learned that her name was Brenda. We talked for a minute, and I found out that she needed the pistol because she was at the other end of Blackstone selling crack. She then asked me if I wanted to bring some rocks down to her the next day.

That's how my relationship with Brenda began. You know, "Boy meets girl, girl asks boy to borrow a gun, boy and girl start dealing crack together."

Over the next couple of weeks, Brenda and I spoke whenever we saw each other, but she was in hustle mode and not trying to make sparks fly. But one day, I was coming down the block when I noticed Brenda in a different way. She had her hair done, a little makeup on, and was dressed in a cute short set, looking like a young lady. Her face was glowing, and instead of the serious look she normally wore, she had a smile on her face. She had piqued my interest, and according to one of my homegirls, I too had piqued hers. Within a few days, our brief conversations grew in length, and we started hanging out together.

On the exterior, Brenda had been hardened by the streets of Brightmoor and a rough upbringing. She would fight without much provocation, and she wasn't afraid to stand her ground. However, the more I got to know her, the more I saw a young lady with a big heart. She would do anything she could to make sure her siblings had money, food, and clothing, and she would fight to the bloody end if anyone threatened them. Sadly, however, like many Black youth growing up in dysfunctional homes, her golden heart had been callused by neglect, hurt, and heartbreak.

At the start of our relationship, we would spend most of our time hanging out, laughing and joking, or kicking it in the back room of her family's house. It wasn't long, though, before the mercurial nature of our personalities began to clash. I was raised to respect women and treat them well, but nothing in the father-son handbook had prepared me to deal with a girl as volatile as Brenda. She didn't believe in holding her tongue, whether she was right or wrong, and I refused to be spoken to in a disrespectful manner. The first argument we had—over my refusal to loan her sister money for an outfit—nearly came to blows, and I should have known then that we were in for a bumpy ride. Together, we were like two birds with broken wings, trying to find solace in each other.

By the next month, Brenda and I had moved in together and were selling crack out of our house, doing whatever we felt was necessary to survive. We had customers coming to the same place we laid our heads, so we were extra vigilant. We were careful about who we let in to buy from us, and we kept several guns in the house, never doubting whether either of us would use one if necessary. We had both seen enough to know that no one was to be trusted. At any given moment, a customer could become an enemy, or a rival dealer might try to set us up.

It was a fast, hard life characterized by desperation and hopelessness. With each day, I drank more and more in an effort to numb myself from the madness around me. I was tired of seeing crack-addicted parents selling food and clothes that should've been going to their children. I was tired of defending our territory from other dealers. I wasn't happy, and no matter how much money we made, it wasn't enough to heal the deep wounds I had suffered as a kid.

The spring months came and went rapidly. Our days and nights started merging together into a blur of trips to Northland Mall, meals at fast-food restaurants, and impromptu parties at cheap motels. Like most dealers, we were living for the moment. We had no plans to get out of the game or do anything responsible with our earnings. We spent money as fast as we made it, and we were always playing catch-up. If we had stopped to notice how little money we were left with, we would've discovered that we were risking our lives for what amounted to a minimum-wage job.

After a few months, business began to pick up when I started an operation with Brenda's cousin's boyfriend, who had been selling from another spot at the other end of the neighborhood and had a couple of thousand dollars saved up. We went in together on various amounts of crack and cocaine, and split the profits, which helped us go from making a few hundred dollars a day to making a couple thousand every few days. It wasn't kingpin status, but we felt like we were moving in the right direction.

The timing couldn't have been better, because Brenda thought she was pregnant. She was developing all of the usual signs—morning sickness, mood swings, and weird eating habits. At night, we would lie in bed kicking it about our child and the dreams we had for him or her. Knowing that a new life would soon come into our world, we changed our approach to hustling and began talking about saving enough money to leave the game, move away, and make a fresh start. But, although we spent most nights talking about our grand plans for our new life together, when the morning came, it was right back to business as usual.

Brenda and I really did want better for ourselves and our child; we just didn't know how to escape the pull of what had become a vicious cycle of crime and desperation. And it wouldn't be long before that cycle claimed me for good.

16

MICHIGAN REFORMATORY
Ionia, Michigan
1994

It was my second time being sent to solitary confinement at the Michigan Reformatory, but this time around, I was more aware of what to expect, and how to manage being caged up for twenty-three hours a day. I quickly developed a routine of sleeping through the morning and reading late into the night as the other inmates caused mayhem up and down the tier.

Thirty days into this stretch, my father came up to see me. We tried having a normal conversation, and he did everything in his power to comfort me with warm words and thoughts from home. He meant well, but all the conversation did was remind me of how I would never stand on free soil again.

On the outside, life was continuing on without me. My little sisters were becoming young women. Brenda was struggling to raise Li'l Jay as a single mother, and my son would become a teenager and a young man without ever getting a chance to throw a football with me.

After about six months in the hole, I was released back to general population. I was assigned to a job in the kitchen but soon got fired for getting in an argument with my supervisor. This gave me more time to build with the brothers on the yard. We formed coalitions and intense study groups with other organizations, and one day, the brothers nominated me to become a spiritual advisor. I was now responsible for the spiritual growth and direction of the brothers in our organization. I would be the main speaker at each service, and I would serve as a counselor, helping the brothers to navigate through whatever emotional and spiritual challenges they faced. I was now also responsible for all communication between our brotherhood and the leaders of the other religious organizations.

I hadn't ever thought of becoming a spiritual advisor, but it turned out that I was a natural for the position. I started challenging the board of directors to think of different ways to educate the brothers. Our old model of having members commit literature to memory had proven ineffective, so I created study guides that would help the brothers better understand the material. I also helped the members become more disciplined when it came to standing up to the officers on the yard. Instead of the Bible and the Quran, which we used for spiritual development, I encouraged the brothers to read more revolutionary literature by authors like Assata Shakur and George Jackson.

Not long after leaving the kitchen, I was given a job working in the recreation center, which was the heartbeat of the joint. Every hustle imaginable took place there, from drug trafficking and loan sharking to gambling and playing pool for money. It was the perfect job for me as the spiritual advisor, because it gave me access to every yard. I could set up meetings whenever I wanted under the guise of a basketball or weight-lifting callout, and whenever we had a beef on the yard, we were able to coordinate and strategize in a way that allowed us to retaliate with stealth.

As our battles with other inmates intensified and hits were ordered, I found myself battling the same contradictions I had felt at Standish. On one hand, I was teaching the brothers that white supremacy and fascism were the enemy, but in the next breath, I was ordering the stabbings of other inmates—inmates who had brown flesh like me.

I grew tired of being forced to respond and retaliate anytime a beef sprang up (which at the Gladiator School was a regular occurrence). Eventually, the weight on my shoulders grew so great that I decided to resign my post and step back to reassess where I was headed in life. I was growing in my consciousness, but the gravitational pull of prison life was overwhelming. I found myself in a constant internal battle, and the only time I felt at peace was when I was in the recreation center working out.

It was around this time that I wrote an article for the prison newspaper about my sister's battle with crack addiction and how it made me feel. I didn't give it much thought, but a month or so later, the article prompted a conversation that would change the course of my life.

When I arrived at work one day, I found our supervisor Tom sitting in the recreation center reading the paper. He kept looking up from the newspaper and then at me, with a curiosity that I hadn't recognized before.

"Shaka, did you really write this?" he asked.

"Yeah, I wrote it, Tom," I said with a chuckle.

"This is really good, Shaka. I want to take it home and share it with my wife."

The next day he told me that his wife, who was a magazine

editor, thought I had a future as a writer. I had never thought of writing as something to be taken seriously. I was serious about reading, of course, but the only future I could dream of was one where I simply got out of prison and went on with my life. I had never thought of becoming anything other than free.

But Tom's words stayed with me. It had been a long time since someone had said something affirming about me that wasn't connected to violence. It made me feel like I could be good at something other than hustling drugs and hurting people.

WITHIN SIX MONTHS, I had firmly established my position in the prison. The inmates counted on me to be fair, and one of the things that separated me from others was my diplomacy. In the midst of conflict, I always tried to find a way for us all to get what we wanted in the end. I wanted my money and they wanted their lives, so more often than not, we were able to work something out.

During the summer of 1996, things started heating up between several of the organizations and the officers. We were tired of two officers in particular. They ran the yard at the Reformatory, and in the preceding weeks had slammed several inmates to the ground and illegally confiscated property that they had no right to take. We organized silent protests, unified workout regimens, and employed other tactics to let them know that we stood together. Officers retaliated by setting up some of the leaders from our organizations, and I found myself on the receiving end of their harassment.

An officer named Sergeant W. started shaking me down every chance he got and destroying my cell on a daily basis. I never got caught slipping, but eventually, he got me transferred to Carson City Correctional Facility, to separate me from the brothers I had been helping to organize. In my absence, though, the war at the Reformatory waged on. Not long after I transferred, several officers were jumped, and one was nearly stabbed to death.

MY MOVE TO Carson City would mark the beginning of a three-year period of back-to-back transfers from prison to prison. I spent eleven months at Carson City, another year at Oaks Correctional in Manistee, and a year or so at Gus Harrison Correctional in Adrian, where there was a lot of racial tension between the inmates and guards. Each of these prisons looked the same—large, red-brick buildings that resembled recreation centers—the go-to template during Michigan's prison boom.

At each stop, I became close with the Melanic brothers, working to educate the young guys and build common ground with the other organizations at the prison. I also intensified our physical training to ensure that we were balanced in our development. We would make what we called a "cook up" and eat together nearly every day, to make sure all of the brothers were getting their basic nutrition. The cook up was a concoction made of ramen noodles, cheese, summer sausage, pickles, and chili poured over nachos. It was our way of supplementing meals from the chow hall and breaking up the monotony of the prison slop that they fed us.

By the time I transferred to Adrian, I was eight years into my sentence and beginning to see the light at the end of the tunnel. I was halfway through the minimum range of my sentence, and I had worked hard to decrease my security level. One day, my father, son, and stepmother came to visit, and I shared with them the excitement I felt knowing that I was steadily working my way through my sentence and would be in medium security soon. My father told me that he was proud of me for handling myself and staying out of trouble. I still had eight years until my earliest release date, but it felt good to know that I had made it through the first half of my sentence.

There would be light at the end of the tunnel for me, indeed—but that's not what would come first. A few days after that visit, the administration decided to break up the leadership of our organization, and they transferred me to a prison in Muskegon. It was there that everything I had learned would be put to the test. A test that I would fail.

17

BRIGHTMOOR
West Side Detroit
1991

One hot summer day in July, Brenda and I were sitting in the living room when our friend Derrick stopped by and asked me to DJ a party that was happening that weekend. It had been forever since I had touched a turntable, but I said yes. Music was one of my passions, and I loved nothing more than watching people dance to whatever symphony I had composed. Brenda and I spent all week looking forward to the night, and we even took a trip to the mall to make sure we would look fresh for the occasion.

We arrived at the party early, but people had already started showing up—a good sign that the night was going to be live. Within an hour or so, the backyard was packed and the celebration was in full swing. Everyone was drinking and smoking, but I was taking it easy because I didn't want to get too drunk while I was spinning. That didn't last long, though, because a few of my homeboys from another 'hood soon came through and started passing around Olde English "800" and Seagram's gin. I knew my limits, so I let someone else take over the turntables and went to drink with my crew.

We had a table in the back of the yard, and Brenda and I started dancing and acting silly with each other. It was the first time we had been to a party together, and we were having the time of our lives.

Then the gunshots rang out.

People started running out of the backyard, screaming and hollering. I pulled out my pistol and told everybody in our crew to follow me to the front of the house. When we got there, one of my homeboys found me and explained what had happened. "Man, that nigga Derrick just shot a motherfucker in the chest." Derrick was in our crew, so if he was the one doing the shooting, it meant that we had better be on the lookout, too.

I didn't know what was going on. The beef could have been with someone we didn't know, and he could've been on his way back to retaliate. Or it could've been with someone we knew, and who knew where to find us. It hadn't been long since I'd been shot, and I didn't like knowing that someone might come to my house and retaliate for what Derrick had done.

Derrick was nowhere to be found, so I had no way of gauging the situation. I told Brenda that it was best for us to head home, and we started walking back around the corner to our house. On the way there, I was paranoid, looking over my shoulder with every other step and keeping my eyes out for headlights.

As we turned the corner onto our block, a Jeep pulled up to our side. I eased my finger around the trigger of the .380 in my pocket, planning to shoot through my jeans if I saw any sign of beef— but it turned out that the driver was only looking for directions.

I breathed a sigh of relief and continued talking to Brenda as we walked up the driveway to the front of our house.

Just as we were opening the door to go inside, a nondescript white sedan pulled up out front. The driver slowly lowered his window, and all I could think about was how vulnerable we were, there on the porch without anything to use for cover. Once again, I found my finger resting in the crook of the trigger in my pocket.

Then a familiar voice called out from the backseat of the car. "Yo, Jay, you on?"

It was Tom, one of my favorite customers. Tom was a middle-aged white dude from a West Side suburb called Novi. He talked slick and fast like he was from the 'hood, and he was known to spend several hundred dollars each time he stopped by.

The sound of Tom's familiar voice eased my nerves, so I told Brenda to go inside and started walking over to the car. My friend and partner in crime Mark followed close behind.

When I reached the car, I saw two unfamiliar white men sitting in the front seat. Tom was in the back, holding more money than I had ever seen him carry. It didn't look right.

"Yo, why you bringing people I don't know to my house," I said to Tom. "You know the rules over here."

"They're cool, Jay," Tom said. "We just want to get a package. Why are you acting so uptight?"

Tom and I started arguing. I told Tom that it looked like he was trying to make a deal for the police, and I wasn't going to serve him. He continued begging, trying to convince me to hook him up, but I was irritated and paranoid, and I just wanted the night to be over. It was time for this conversation to end.

"You got five minutes to get off of the block before things get bad," I said.

This time, it was Tom's friend who replied. "It's a free country," he said. "And we don't have to go anywhere."

This put me even more on edge than before. "If you know what's good for you," I said, "you'd get the fuck from over here." My voice was getting louder and more menacing, but Tom's friend wouldn't back down.

"Fuck you, we not leaving until we get what we came for," he shot back.

I had never seen a customer come in the 'hood and act so brazen. "Are y'all the police?" I asked, and told them again to leave. But Tom's friend continued shouting out of the car.

"What the fuck you mean are we the police? We came to spend money and you acting all tough and shit. You ain't that fucking tough!" he screamed. It was too dark for me to make out the features of his face, but I could see him leaning forward in the passenger's seat like he was about to jump out of the car. That's when I pulled out my pistol.

Mark, who had been watching the whole scene unfold, jumped in to calm things down. "Fuck them, Jay, let's go in. They not talking about shit, and it ain't worth getting caught up." We turned and started walking toward the house.

Then, suddenly, Tom's friend opened the car door. Something in me snapped. Memories of getting shot flashed through my head, and every one of my instincts screamed that it was about to happen again. I spun back around with the pistol in my hand.

Tom's friend said something else, but to this day, I can't remember what it was. I'm not sure I even heard him. All I recall is the feeling of danger that surged through me as I fired several shots—*BANG! BANG! BANG!*—into the car. The tires screeched as they sped off down the block and around the corner.

I never saw the guy's face—never saw if he had anything in his hand or not. I hadn't heard him yell out in pain, and I didn't know where the shots I fired had landed. But something in my soul told me that a terrible thing had happened. In that moment, I knew the guy had died. I had shot several people before, but only to scare them off. This time was different; this time, I had shot to kill.

When I went back into the house, everyone looked at me like I was a ghost. Their faces were solemn and their eyes were accusatory, as if they knew the shots had been fatal, too. I saw a level of fear in their faces that had never been there before. Brenda and I decided to pack up, lock the house down, and go spend the night at her cousin's house.

When we got there, I told Brenda that I knew I had killed the man, and she broke down crying in my arms. The consequences of our life on the streets had finally hit home, and in the worst way. Here was Brenda, pregnant and ready for a brighter future together, and I had done something that promised to rob our little family of any hope of a better life. I had helped to bring a new life into the world—but now I was taking my life out of it.

FOR YEARS, the circumstances of my arrest were a focal point of my bitterness.

The day after the shooting, a detective showed up at my door, and I learned that everyone I thought of as a friend had turned his or her back on me. In my naïveté, I had expected them to stay true to the code of the streets, but when the officers came knocking, every last one of them made a statement against me. In the police station at 1300 Beaubien, I hung my head in shame as the officers read statement after statement, driving home the reality that my friends had given me up. I felt betrayed—but what the hell did I know about right and wrong? I had just killed a man over a meaningless argument.

I was a fool, and had been one for a long time. Each time I

had hit the block to hustle, I was putting my life in someone else's hands. Each time I had carried a gun under the influence of alcohol, I was taking the chance that something could go horribly wrong. Each time I had talked about getting my life in order, only to go back to the streets, I was rolling the dice and gambling with my future.

Now I was charged with open murder in a case that I had no chance of winning. The game was over, and I had no future left to gamble.

18

MUSKEGON CORRECTIONAL FACILITY
Muskegon, Michigan
1999

Among the inmates in Michigan's prison system, Muskegon Correctional Facility had earned a reputation as one of the best places you could be transferred. It was one of the only prisons in Michigan that allowed inmates to ride bikes, play golf, and hang out almost anywhere in the prison. Ironically, it also had a reputation as one of the most dangerous facilities, because guys there would get too comfortable and forget that, despite the relaxed environment, they were still in prison.

I arrived in the sweltering heat of summer and was assigned to a double cell with a brother who was days away from going home. When he told me that he would be getting out in a few weeks, a small knot grew in my stomach. While I was happy to see a brother leaving, I was saddened by the reality that I wouldn't be walking out of those doors behind him. This was why I had long ago blocked out thoughts of what it would be like to be released from prison—it was the only way I could keep myself from going insane.

I eased back into my regular routine of working out, studying, and building with the brothers at that prison. I enrolled in an automotive tech class, and my life seemed to be moving in a positive direction.

The summer was moving along quickly, and our Melanic brotherhood was preparing for our annual Day of Remembrance celebration, where we honored the memory and legacy of the millions of Africans who were enslaved or died during the transatlantic slave trade. We fasted for twenty-four hours in preparation for our annual banquet in the chow hall, where we would reflect on our ancestors and the opportunities we had to make a positive contribution to the world.

At the ceremony, I gave a passionate speech about the sacrifices made by our prophet Nat Turner in his attempt to liberate our ancestors from bondage. Many of the brothers had already admired Turner for the bravery that empowered him to take up arms against his slave masters, but I reminded them that his greatest sacrifice was risking his life to learn how to read, which in turn had made him a better leader. For the brothers who had grown up in the 'hood, it was a revelation to hear that the written word was as powerful a weapon as a loaded gun.

When the ceremony ended, some of the younger brothers began gravitating toward me. They told me that they respected my balance and integrity, and they had never heard anyone use history to help them understand what was happening to them in the present. They were inspired to learn more so that they, too, could lead and make a difference when they were released.

By that point in my sentence, I had grown tired of the challenges that came with being part of an organization—from negotiating with the officers to clashing with the elder brothers who were stuck in the old mindset of "might makes right"—but these conversations with the younger brothers fueled my desire to make a difference in the brotherhood.

As fall arrived, I was feeling good about things. The cool air always made me feel optimistic. It was a symbol that the year was coming to an end and a new one was beginning, which meant I had knocked another year off of my sentence. Freedom was beginning to feel more tangible, and I clung to anything I could use as a sign of good things to come (like Serena Williams claiming her first U.S. Open title on September 12, 1999). I could feel myself becoming a leader, a deep thinker, and a man of self-control—the kind of man that my readings of African history had inspired me to become.

That is, until one fateful day in October, when everything I had learned over the last eight years was put on the line.

THE DAY STARTED off normal enough, or at least as normal as a day in prison could be. I went to breakfast, and then to class. When I walked into the classroom, a few of the guys were sitting around, joking about who was going to fail an upcoming exam. "You know Shaka ole smart ass gonna pass the damn test and make the rest of us look bad," one guy said, causing the whole class to laugh.

That afternoon, as I was walking back from my automotive technology class, I felt like my bladder was about to explode. I knew that the officers were about to do count, so I was rushing to make it to the bathroom before they locked us down for the next hour and a half. We didn't have toilets in our cells, so using the common bathroom was the only option I had.

Suddenly, the shriek of the siren filled our unit. This was the signal for our monthly emergency count, during which we all had to drop whatever it was we were doing and return to our cells. I quickened my pace. I didn't have much time, but I knew that if I hurried upstairs, I could get to the bathroom in time to relieve myself before lockdown.

When I reached the top of the stairs, I saw several inmates scurrying in and out of the bathroom, and my heart dropped when I noticed the officer who was standing at the door. This particular officer disliked me because, a few days earlier, he and I had gotten into a heated verbal exchange when he refused to let me onto the yard after my class got out early. I cited the prison's policy, which said I was in the right, and he backed down—but I knew that my stand wouldn't come without a price. I figured he would, at a minimum, go and shake my cell down and throw my meager belongings around. (Which happened right on schedule, the very next day.)

This wasn't the first time I had witnessed this superiority complex that white officers carry on their chest like badges. In fact, even the officers who professed to have no racial prejudices were prone to exact revenge on a Black inmate if they thought he had gotten over on them. I had been working every day to better myself and learn how to resolve conflict through the proper channels, but I realized that this rubbed a lot of officers the wrong way. And now the same officer I had embarrassed was standing at the door to the bathroom.

As I approached the door, he stopped me and said, "Hey, where are you going?" The tone of his voice made it clear that he wasn't going to let me in.

I told him that I needed to use the bathroom, but he looked me in the eye and said, "No, I don't think so." Meanwhile, other inmates were walking in and out of the bathroom, unimpeded.

I had two choices in that moment: I could either accept a minor misconduct for disobeying a direct order, or I could go back to my cell and urinate on myself or out the window. The latter felt like an insult to my dignity, so I brushed past the officer and entered the bathroom. The few inmates who were in there hurried out—they had heard about my confrontations with officers at other prisons and knew that things could get ugly real quick.

"That's an assault on staff," the officer barked as I relieved myself at the urinal. He was lying. I knew he could charge me with disobeying a direct order, but I hadn't assaulted him. If I had, he would have immediately pushed his Personal Protection Device, to alert the other officers that he was in danger.

As I flushed the urinal and walked over to wash my hands, the officer and I exchanged glances.

"Give me your ID," he demanded, standing in the doorway to block my exit from the bathroom.

"I don't have my ID on me," I said in as calm a voice as I could muster. "It's in my cell."

He asked me several more times for my ID, and I told him each time that I didn't have it. He smiled sardonically, which made me realize that this was a game he was enjoying immensely. No matter how many times he asked me for my ID, I couldn't give him what I didn't have. He reminded me of a schoolyard bully who continues to shake the life out of a kid even after the kid tells him over and over that he doesn't have any lunch money.

A few inmates were still crowded around the door, trying to watch what was going on. They pleaded with the officer to let me out of the bathroom, but he responded by ordering them to lock up. He then turned back to me and continued to egg me on.

"You'll produce an ID or you won't leave out of here," he warned, stepping close enough for me to feel his hot breath on my face. It felt like the whole world was closing in on me. I attempted to slide past the officer, but he pushed me in the chest, demanding again that I produce an ID.

Maybe it was the officer's display of dominance, maybe it was the built-up frustration from being mistreated by guards for the last eight years, but something in me snapped. All I could hear was the word "nigger" echoing over and over in my head, telling me that I was a piece of shit and that my personal space could be violated at will. I felt cornered. I thought of all the Black men I had read about, the ones who had been dragged from their beds in the middle of the night kicking and screaming, their cries silenced by the thick rope that was wrapped tightly around their necks. I thought of all the Black women who had been raped in slave quarters while their husbands stood by helplessly, holding in all of their rage to keep their families from being brutally beaten or murdered.

In one smooth leap, I attacked the officer, punching him in the face and neck several times and knocking him to the ground. Then I scooped him up and slammed him on his back, all the while continuing to punch him. With each smashing blow, a weight seemed to lift. I was no one's slave, and it was better to die or spend the rest of my life in prison than allow someone—officer or not—to trample on my dignity.

By the time another officer managed to twist my hands behind my back, I felt liberated. Several guards dragged the officer I had attacked—who was now unconscious—into the bathroom. Meanwhile, two other officers cuffed me and began escorting me to the hole.

As I was led away, I looked around at the inmates who had stood by watching the whole thing play out. Their eyes were full of contempt and anger, but I was shocked to see that it wasn't directed at the officer who had bullied me. It was all directed at me. I looked into the eyes of some of the Melanic brothers who were there. These were men that I had vowed to defend and lay my life down for, but now they lowered their heads and walked away in silence. I felt condemned by my brothers, and that was far worse than anything the state could do to me.

The officers led me down to the hole and told me that I was being placed on long-term segregation. It wasn't news to me—I had been sent there before, and for far less serious crimes. But this time, it wouldn't be a temporary arrangement. This time, I would stay in the hole for four and a half years.

PART THREE

19

OAKS CORRECTIONAL FACILITY
Manistee, Michigan
October 1999

If there's one thing I remember about the cell that I inhabited for four and a half years, it's the smell. Throughout the unit, the stench of defecation, of rotting feet, of unwashed armpits and un-washed asses mingled with the lingering cloud of pepper spray. It pervaded everything, from the air to your clothes and the sheets on your bed, and it will forever be burned in my memory as the smell of human despair.

I had begun that day in the hole back at Muskegon. As I sat on the bed, thinking about the inmates who had betrayed me, I wondered if Nat Turner had felt what I felt when two slaves turned him in to his slave master. I wondered if Malcolm X felt the way I did as he took his last breath, bleeding out from gunshot wounds inflicted by the very people he was trying to save. I thought about all of my ancestors who had taken a stand for justice, only to have their own people turn their backs on them.

Within two hours, several officers came to my cell and told me to back up to the door so that they could handcuff and shackle me. I was being transferred. The guards hustled me out to a waiting van, which shuttled me an hour and a half north to Oaks Maximum Correctional Facility. It would be my second trip to Oaks, but my first experience serving time in the hole there.

When I arrived in the control center, several officers stood around in a small circle, holding handcuffs and shackles. The officers who had brought me in needed to get their cuffs back, so they were forced to use a complicated maneuver that would allow them to switch the cuffs without freeing my hands and feet in the process.

The switch with the handcuffs went smoothly, but when they got down to the shackles, they discovered that the officer at Muskegon had placed the shackles on upside down, making it difficult to get the key into the lock. An officer attempted to twist the shackles around so that he could see better, but that caused the metal to bite into the tender flesh on the back of my ankles. After a few frustrating minutes, another officer decided to kick the shackles, which caused them to sink deeper into my flesh.

We exchanged glares, and I said the first words I had uttered since leaving Muskegon:

"If you put your feet on me again, I guarantee I will put you in a hospital bed next to your colleague."

The officer glared at me in silence, but he didn't kick the shackles again. He and his partners finished making the switch and escorted me down to the block where my new cell was located.

I was immediately placed in a shower cage and strip-searched, then taken to a temporary segregation cell. As the officers opened the cage, they threatened to slam me to the ground if I made any sudden movements. I did what they said, standing still as they searched me, but on the inside, I was laughing. Beneath the guards' bravado was a fact that I knew made them very uncomfortable: They were terrified of me. In my prior conflicts with officers, I knew they had to have been somewhat afraid, but this time was different. I could sense the fear leaping from their bodies.

Over the next couple days, I felt like an animal in a zoo exhibit. Officer after officer came to my cell, hoping to get a glimpse of this "monster" they had heard so much about. Word had circulated throughout the prison system that I had nearly beaten an officer to death at Muskegon, and that I was suspected of having ordered hits on inmates and officers at my previous stops.

As the officers filed past my cell to gawk at me, neither they nor I could guess how much our perception of each other would change over the next four and a half years. In fact, this day would mark the beginning of a very powerful transformation inside of me, one that would see me begin to confront my demons and recover the humanity I had lost during all those years of violence, anger, and pain.

But to get there, I would first have to go through Michigan's version of hell on earth.

THE TIERS SMELLED and sounded of gloom. Each wing of the four-wing unit had twenty or so spartan cells, each containing only a concrete slab for a bed and a steel toilet and sink.

Within a few weeks, I would be introduced to a whole new language and culture of madness. Each day I was awakened to the sounds of footlockers being banged shut nonstop. I couldn't tell which cells the noise was coming from, but the sound was deafening, stopping only when an officer would run up on the tier. Once the banging stopped, the officers would serve breakfast and ask us if we wanted to go out for our yard period, which amounted to five hour-long sessions a week in a cage that resembled a dog kennel.

After yard, the unit would simmer down, and I would pace the floor as I listened to the other inmates play chess by hollering out their moves beneath their cell doors. They would use the back of notepads to make chessboards, and they tore paper into small bits that they could use as pieces. The games were very competitive, and were often gambled on by other inmates, who would pay up in the only currency we had in the hole: toiletries and stamped envelopes. In these quieter moments on the tier, it was fascinating to hear the other inmates calling out their moves—but the quiet moments didn't last for long.

You'd think that enclosing inmates within their own cells for twenty-three hours a day would minimize conflict, but even in the hole, beefs formed constantly over gambling debts, arguments over religious views, and inmates who had butted into conversations that weren't meant for them. In an attempt to gain a semblance of control over their environment, the inmates would take these slights as opportunities to wage battle with each other and the officers.

The weapon of choice was what we called "weapons of ass destruction." These feces-filled bottles were smuggled to the showers or yard cages, where they could be deployed like water pistols on unsuspecting victims. If they couldn't get you in that way, they would make shit patties and slide them underneath your door. (I stayed out of this. I had no interest in playing with my own feces, and I sure as hell wasn't going to risk subjecting myself to the bodily fluids of another inmate.)

One day, two inmates were arguing over an unpaid gambling debt, and one of them manipulated his food slot open, waiting for one of the officers to escort his enemy to the shower. When the two of them walked by, he kicked the food slot open and squirted a thick stream of feces from his colostomy bag onto the inmate and the officer. The smell of shit hung in the air like a miasmic cloud for the next couple of days.

For every measure of prevention that the officers came up with, the inmates devised a way around it. At one point, they drilled bolts into the food slots to keep the inmates from being able to open them, but several inmates went into MacGyver mode trying to figure out a way to jimmy the locks. It didn't take long. First, they slid a comb attached to a piece of string over the top of their door, with their across-the-hall neighbor guiding their movements. Once the comb was lined up with the bolt, they would pull up on it until the lock came undone. After that, all they had to do was slide a cable cord beneath the door, twist it around the knob, and continue twisting until the slot popped open and the weapons of ass destruction could be employed again.

Another weapon in the hole was sleep deprivation. Sometimes when inmates were in conflict with each other, they'd beat on the steel toilets or walls all night with a brush or the hard plastic shower shoes we had been given. This, of course, impacted the whole wing, but there was never any regard for innocent bystanders, and this often led to others being drawn into the wars. Within moments of the lights going out, the tier would erupt with the sound of multiple toilets being banged on and men hollering and screaming through the cracks beneath their cell doors. Sometimes the banging would last for weeks, or until one of the culprits was moved to a cell in a different unit. Another method of getting even was to blow the power in your neighbor's cell by shoving a staple into your electrical outlet. The three inmates who shared your breaker would lose power, which would keep them from being able to watch the three channels of TV that we had.

I was terrified by the depth of the psychosis that I witnessed on a daily basis. From the guy beating on his door to the man down the hall who took a magazine staple and ripped his scrotum open, or my neighbor who would cut himself and destroy his cell in a rage, I got to the point where I could no longer tell who was crazy. The staff psychiatrist claimed that these inmates were just "acting out," but during my years in the hole, I had learned that isolation causes a disconnect in the deepest part of the human psyche. The feeling of being alone, vulnerable, and unable to make real decisions was suffocating, and the monotony of being in a small cell without normal human contact or face-to-face interactions could drive even the most well-behaved inmate to the brink of insanity. There is nothing humane about being caged in a cell for twenty-three hours a day, and when you add this to all of the other stresses that inmates face—the torture of regrets from your past, the neglect and abandonment from your family members—you have a surefire recipe for disaster.

One night, a Latino inmate chose to end his life. His ordeal had begun weeks before, when the officers began harassing him constantly because of his sexual orientation. On a daily basis, I would hear the officers call him names like "dick-sucking fuckboy" and "queer booty bandit."

One night, he woke everyone up with a loud and chilling rendition of the Lord's Prayer. It freaked us out, but this was just a warm-up for the next day, when he set the cell on fire while he was inside. As the inmate's screams filled the cellblock, officers rushed onto the wing, opened his door, and hosed him down with a fire extinguisher before taking him to suicide watch for twenty-four hours. Within two weeks, he had attempted the same thing again, so they removed him from the cell and never brought him back.

Every day that I spent in the hole, there was something going on that challenged my humanity. There were days when I felt hopeless as I listened to a man across the hall beat senselessly on his door for hours at a time and I couldn't get away from the thoughts and regrets that had plagued me throughout my entire sentence. The worst part was that I had no idea when I would be released from this madhouse.

———

BY THE TIME I had been in the hole for two years, I had grown tired of seeing grown men descending to craziness. I knew that if something didn't change, I would end up just like them. This was when I broke down in front of the mirror, forgiving everyone I had held anger for, all of those years. I was tired of living in a ball of bitterness and rage, and I was tired of hurting people, including myself. For the first time in my life, I was starting to see my anger for what it really was: a destructive force that would tear me apart unless I found a way to change.

But as I sat back listening to the chaos around me, I felt like I had nowhere to turn. The officers had no vested interest in helping me turn my life around. In fact, to most of them, I meant job security—the state had long ago given up the hope that I could be rehabilitated. The other prisoners—well, their talent was for spreading anger and violence, not fostering emotional growth and maturity. It was up to me to become the man and father that I longed to be. So I took a long and painful look at myself, and started the hard work of carving out a sanctuary in the middle of the madness.

I began treating my time in the hole as if I were in school, setting up my cell each morning like a classroom. I ordered more books from the library than ever before and created courses for myself in subjects from political science and African history to religion and psychology. I created quizzes and exams that I would go back to at the end of the week to make sure I was retaining the information. When I wasn't studying or writing, I would read for pleasure late into the night.

But real changes came when I started keeping a journal. Anytime I got angry at one of the other inmates, I would immediately grab a lined notepad and begin writing down what I wanted to do to him and why.

One day, my neighbor blew my power while trying to get a light for his cigarette. When I asked him if he had done it, he lied, and my immediate thought was that I wanted to kill him. To me, he was a worthless piece of shit who deserved a swift and painful death. I wrote these thoughts down and returned to the pages a few days later. When I read what I had written, it disturbed me. The other inmate had been inconsiderate, no doubt, but was it really meant as a personal attack? And even if it was, did he really deserve to be harmed, or even killed, as payback?

It's hard to express how much this process of examination began to change me. Within the lined pages of my notepads, I got in touch with a part of me that didn't feel fear whenever something didn't go my way—a part of me that was capable of feeling compassion for the men around me.

For the first time I could remember, I began to recognize my true self. At the end of the day, I realized that I hadn't been much different from those who used weapons of ass destruction and banged senselessly on their lockers each night. Inside of me burned that same rage—rage that had nearly cost an officer his life and me the rest of my life in prison. Rage that had compelled me to take a man's life while I was on the streets, all those years ago. I thought I had been fighting for my dignity and respect, but I hadn't realized how undignified and disrespectful my anger caused me to be.

As the months passed, I used my journals to document the wars between the inmates and the officers. Whenever the officers did something that we felt was unjust, we would flood the wing with water from our toilets until they cut the water off. The officers knew that if they didn't pass out our mail in a timely fashion, or if they served our meals cold, they would soon be wading through ankle-deep water, trying to get the porters to clean it up. The way we saw it, if we didn't fight back, they would continue to run roughshod over us.

On one of these occasions, as I stood by my door watching the two-inch-deep pool of water ebb and flow outside of my cell, I couldn't help thinking about all the people in Third World countries who were dying because they didn't have clean water. Yet here we were, wasting water as a weapon of war.

Plenty of days, I felt like the hole would consume my spirit. I swore I couldn't take one more day smelling another human being's bodily waste, or one more rejection from the prison's security classification committee regarding my release from administrative segregation. But with pen and paper, I clung to my sanity. I would sit down and write out my thoughts or work through the message of an inspirational book.

I was getting deeper into books on spirituality, faith, and meditation, and these activities helped keep me strong and resolute. I was growing to appreciate Eastern philosophy, with its emphasis on personal accountability and responsibility, and I also resumed reading the Bible and other religious texts, because I realized that spirituality is a common thread that connects all of us to one another.

As I continued to write, I slowly began realizing that I had deep emotional issues that I had never addressed—the biggest one being the hurt from my relationship with my mother. I wrote about how I felt as a child when she would beat me over minor infractions: how vulnerable I was when she forced me to strip before beating me, or when she berated me for something that had been my siblings' fault. At first, these memories filled me with shame— the same shame I felt on the night I had tried to take my own life. But, looking the situation in the face for the first time, I realized I had been carrying guilt that didn't belong to me. I had been a little boy, and regardless of my behavior, no child deserves to hear his mother say, "I'm tired of your nappy-headed ass," or, "I wish you'd never been born."

I wrote about my parents' divorce and the pain it had caused me, discovering that balance and safety were the things I desired most as a child. I began to see the tug-of-war I had played, trying to live up to the expectations of two parents who had very different outlooks on the world. And I began picturing how I would do things differently if I ever got released and had the chance to be a father myself. I knew that my children deserved to grow up with the love and understanding of their parents. I knew that I would never make them feel like they were a burden to me.

I wrote about the physical violence I had suffered in my life, and how it had made me feel toward people. The way I had come to see it, no one had ever felt anything for me, so I didn't have the obligation to care about anybody else. I discovered layers upon layers of scars, from feeling unloved and abandoned, to feeling like no one would ever care for me or stand up in my defense. I discovered that, like many young males who grow up in distressed neighborhoods, I probably suffered from post-traumatic stress disorder. I had suppressed these feelings because there was no one I could talk to about them. I didn't have the tools to process all I had experienced, and those feelings had festered like rotten meat, turning into the source of the violence that had possessed me for all of these years.

Each time I filled a page of my journal, I felt as if a great weight had been lifted. No longer did I feel the old familiar bitterness; I was learning a new way to get it out. No longer did I need to carry my anger around inside of me in a tight little ball, keeping me one provocation away from an explosion.

I also wrote books. The first was a novel called *Shadowatchers*. It was about a group of young men and women who vow to make their neighborhood a better place after speaking to the ghosts of famous civil rights figures like Rosa Parks and Malcolm X. I also penned a novel called *Flagrant Foul*, which followed the story of a young woman who is sent to prison after getting into her boyfriend's car that turned out to be loaded with drugs.

With each day that passed, I could feel myself growing stronger and stronger. The pain from years of abuse and neglect began to dissipate, and my feelings toward my fellow inmates started to soften. I stopped shaming my neighbor, who had a smoking habit that he couldn't afford, and began slipping him a cigarette whenever he ran out. I even began to embrace the very inmates who made life on our block a living hell, counseling them and helping them navigate their way through their emotions. We would lie on the floor and talk beneath our doors or through our power sockets, sharing our thoughts on life and the struggles we were going through.

Each day in the hole was a test of my will to survive, as the insanity continued to unfold around me, but the act of writing about the things I saw helped to take away their power.

THE OTHER THING that kept me sane was writing letters to my family. I had written them letters in general population, but being in solitary was a different experience. I was beginning to change and truly grow for the first time in my life, and I was excited to share what I was learning with my father, my siblings, and the friends I loved most. Sometimes I wouldn't get a letter in return, but it didn't stop me from writing. I needed to get my thoughts and feelings out, and when I was sitting at my desk writing, it made me feel connected to the other person, even if only for an hour.

Writing these letters made me remember the first time my son wrote me, four years into my incarceration. He was four years old at the time, and my father had mailed the letter off for him. It was written on the same green paper with the same thick black pencil that I had used as a child. I don't remember the details of what he wrote, but I'll always remember what was written at the bottom of the page:

"I love you daddy."

Those four words pressed on my heart like boulders. I felt like a cheat. I hadn't done one thing to earn Li'l Jay's love. Not once had I stayed up late at night feeding him a warm bottle of milk. Not once had I changed a diaper full of his poop, rocked him to sleep, or sat by his bed to read him a story. His love was something I had not earned.

We continued to write each other over the years, all the while growing closer and closer. I watched in amazement as Li'l Jay transformed from a curious toddler into a scholarly young man who took care of himself and treated others with respect. But the day I truly came to appreciate his growth came three years into this time in the hole, when Li'l Jay sent the most important letter I would ever receive.

WHEN THE SECOND-SHIFT officer slid a bundle of letters beneath my door, I had no idea how my life was about to change I had taken steps to change my life through reading and journaling, but I still felt like something was missing. I had learned to not act on my anger and fear, but I still felt those impulses. And the reality was, I was still in prison, and if I wanted to survive, I needed to act according to the "law of the jungle" that governed prison life.

I swooped up the bundle of mail and rifled through the letters to see who had taken the time to connect with me. There was a letter from a friend at another prison, one from my father, and last, a letter from Li'l Jay.

By then, my son was ten years old, and the sight of an envelope addressed in his squiggly handwriting filled my spirit with joy. I hastily read the two other letters, then sat down to relish the one from my son. But as I tore open the envelope and began reading, I saw that this letter was different from the ones he had sent before.

In the top right-hand corner, Li'l Jay had written in big, capital letters:

MY MOM TOLD ME WHY YOU'RE IN JAIL, BECAUSE OF MURDER! DON'T KILL DAD PLEASE THAT IS A SIN. JESUS WATCHES WHAT YOU DO. PRAY TO HIM.

I stared at the small paragraph for what felt like hours. My body trembled violently, and everything inside of me threatened to break in half. For the first time in my incarceration, I was hit with the truth that my son would grow up to see me as a murderer.

I don't know why I hadn't thought about it before. It's not that I was planning to hide my past from my son—it's just that I thought I would be able to sit down and explain it to him when I felt he was mature enough for the conversation. But as I read Li'l Jay's words, reality kicked me in the gut, and the pain of not knowing what to say spread through my body like cancer.

I didn't know the context of the conversation that he had with his mother. Had Brenda sat him down and explained it to him as she tried to explain my absence? Had she told him I was a killer to scare him into being a good boy? Had she told it to him out of anger or frustration?

I didn't know, so I wasn't sure how to respond. The only thing I was sure of was that I had to do everything in my power to turn my life around. It was the only way I could show my son that I was not a monster.

His letter continued:

Dear daddy, I wonder how you're doing in there. I'm doing fine. When I think about you, it makes me feel sad with no daddy around to wake me up and go work out and be strong like you. I have to do it all by myself. It bothers me the way I miss you. I pray and pray one day my prayer may come true and we'll be together 4 life. It's the anger in my heart that hurts me the most without a dad in the house. My mama said I am the man of the house. She tells me I have to take over the anger so I won't be in jail.

These words touched me in places only a child could reach. Li'l Jay's candor made me smile. He had not yet fallen into the adult habits of making excuses and rationalizing bad decisions. He was unhindered by arbitrarily imposed ideas of what was too impolite or embarrassing to share, so he said exactly what he felt.

Each word seemed to scrape away the scar tissue that had formed around my heart. The words tore off my facade of 'hood toughness and prison savvy. My crime was no badge of honor in my son's eyes—it was a scarlet letter that signified how badly I had failed him and the other young Black males in my neighborhood, many of whom would die or spend their lives in prison for trying to emulate me.

When I finished reading, I was scared for Li'l Jay and all of the other young men who had fathers like me—fathers who were languishing away in prison cells while their sons grew up lost and angry. I had acknowledged my guilt years before, but there was a difference between that and accepting responsibility for my actions. My son's words made me take that final step on my road to redemption.

I sat his letter down and grabbed a pen. I owed my son the truth, but more than this, I owed him a father. Tears ran down my face as I began writing back. I told him the whole story. I explained how and why I had come to prison. I explained to him what it felt like to be a confused teenager, drunk on anger and malt liquor. I told him how it felt to be shot at the age of seventeen, and how that feeling had distorted my thinking. I made a vow to him that I would not murder again.

When I finished writing the letter, I was emotionally drained and spiritually exhausted—but I felt better than I had at any other point in my life. Something in me had changed. I no longer needed to rationalize having taken another person's life. The murder I committed was a senseless act of violence that had shattered people's lives and torn families apart, including mine. But I knew in my heart that we could begin to pick up the pieces.

For all of those years, I was consumed by anger. I worried about what would happen if I wasn't around to save my son from going down the same path I had trod. I never would've thought he'd be the one to save me.

20

The porters had picked up the trays from lunch, and the unit was chaotic as usual. A few inmates were banging lockers shut and yelling up and down the tier. Normally, I would have just blocked out the noise, but I couldn't. Not today. I had too much on my mind.

I had been in solitary confinement for four and a half years, and I was waiting to hear if this time the administration would respond positively to my request—my fourth since I had been at Oaks—and release me from the hole.

The first two times, I'd known I didn't stand a chance. The administration took assaults on staff seriously, so if you found yourself on the wrong end of a situation like that, you had better expect to be held in solitary for at least two years. It wasn't until my third year in the hole that I felt I had a real chance, but I was denied then, too. How much I had changed by that point didn't matter.

Today as I waited, the saying "three strikes and you're out" echoed in my head. I knew men who had been in solitary for more than twenty years.

Finally, the counselor arrived at my door and brought the news I had been looking for. "Mr. White, you have been granted a release to general population. I really hope you take advantage of this second chance."

I was beyond shocked. Sure, I had hoped that I would be released, but I never believed the day would actually come.

A week later, they released me from the hole. I did a George Jefferson stroll down the tier, walking out of the building without handcuffs and shackles for the first time in four and a half years.

Once I got to general population, one of the first things I did was get a word processor and go straight to work typing out the books I had written on prison stationery while I was in the hole. By the time I was released, I was on my third novel, a detective story called *Crack*. It was my favorite of the three because it allowed me to take readers on a journey through the underbelly of street life.

Day after day, I pecked away on my five-year-old word processor. Every thirteen pages, the memory would fill up, and I would have to print out all of the pages, clear the memory, and start typing again. I was in a cell by myself, so I was able to sit for eight hours at a time typing. Still, it took several days of working from breakfast to lights-out for me to finish a manuscript.

A couple months later, they reduced the prison's security level to close custody (a security level between medium and maximum security) and put us in cells with double bunks. I was matched up with a brother from Lansing I had heard a lot about. BX and I were a part of the same brotherhood, so we shared a lot of the same views about life. We both worked in the law library, a job BX had taken because he was serving fifty-two to seventy-five years and wanted to spend most of his time researching law. By then, I had four years left before my earliest release date—and it felt like a long wait until I met BX. He and I worked out together and talked about our sons. He was constantly reminding me how important it was for me to get out of prison so I that could use my testimony to make a difference in my community, and those words kept me motivated to stay on the right track.

A few months later, I was transferred to Carson City. I was sad to be leaving BX—but shortly after I arrived at the new spot, there he was, coming through intake and onto my block. BX and I laughed about the coincidence and agreed that there must have been a reason we were relocated to the same joint. We immediately went to work organizing the brothers and facilitating study groups.

This turned out to be important work, because Carson City had a reputation as one of the most racist facilities in the state. The tension was thick enough to slice with a prison shank. The officers bullied the younger inmates by calling them names like "young dumb punks" and "ghetto thugs," and setting them up on bogus misconducts that caused them to lose their privileges. The younger inmates were clueless about how to deal with the situation, but BX and I showed them how to use the grievance system to address whatever issues they had. This made the younger brothers gravitate to us, and we would train with them—physically and mentally—every day. We felt it was our responsibility to do for them what had been done for us when we first entered the system as teenagers.

Later that year, we organized a Kwanzaa program, and after a successful turnout, we were invited by the special activities director (who oversaw the recreation department) to organize events for Black History Month. We convened a small group of brothers and organized weekly events to honor our people's history. We also created a males' rites of passage program, which taught the younger brothers to read, do research, and respond to life from a position of personal responsibility, reciprocity, and respect.

To help implement the program, I reached out to Yusef, Baruti's son, who by then had been home for a few years. He was the first guy I knew who, after getting released from prison, actually followed through on his promise to become an asset to our community. Yusef was excited to hear from me, and he said he and a brother named Kwasi would support us and come speak at our opening event.

When the day finally came to launch the program, I was filled with excitement. I couldn't wait to see Yusef, as it had been nearly ten years since we'd been at the same prison. When I told my comrade Larry X that Yusef was coming up, he got just as excited as I was. We had all grown up in prison together, sharing books and ideas, and now we would have a chance to reunite.

But when I reached the building where our program was to be held, I was met with disappointment. The activities director informed me that Yusef had been denied a clearance to return to the prison because he had spent time at Carson City while he was incarcerated. I was pissed because I knew how much the younger brothers needed to hear his story—to see that it was possible to get out and do something positive with your life.

The activities director told me that even though Yusef couldn't make it, two other members of Helping Our Prisoners Elevate (HOPE) had been approved for our program. HOPE was a small organization, but I admired and respected the hell out of them. They would send free books to men and women in prison, and they also organized family visits to prisons across the state and published a newsletter to keep us updated on what was happening in the community. We didn't have many organizations that looked out for our interests like this, so I was grateful for the work that HOPE did and was eager to volunteer for them as soon as I got out.

That day, I knew that Kwasi would be one of the two HOPE members visiting us, but when the special activities director returned a few minutes later, I learned that Kwasi had brought with him a beautiful sister named Ebony. Although she and I had exchanged correspondence related to HOPE before, I had never seen her in person. She had beautiful almond-shaped eyes, bright and radiant skin, and long locks that flowed down her back. She was dressed casually, but her model-like looks couldn't be denied, and she gave off a positive aura that made me smile inside.

I welcomed Kwasi and Ebony into the room, where about twenty-five brothers had gathered. The presentations focused on what we would need to do to become difference makers in our communities once we were released. A Q&A session concluded the program, and it was during this session that I developed an intense attraction to Ebony.

She was passionate about her views on Black men and their role in the community. "Our community needs you brothers to return as strong men, teachers, leaders, and mentors for the children who are growing up looking up to you," she said to the crowd of young men. "So, while you are here, do everything you can to change your life."

She articulated her views with a fiery intensity. Her energy made me think of Assata Shakur, who to me epitomized the strength and resilience of Black women. Over the years, I had suppressed my desire to be in the presence of a beautiful woman; I didn't want to be let down by the cold reality of my isolated existence. But those desires returned with a vengeance that day as I listened to Ebony.

I fought the urge to stare at her and drink in all of her beauty. No matter how beautiful Ebony was, I knew I had to tuck away my thoughts for my own sanity and the sake of the program.

A FEW DAYS later, I was moved over to a Level Two unit, also known as medium custody. Level Two was a lot different from Level Four. The units were left open most of the day, and we had keys to our cells. This arrangement allowed us to come and go as we pleased, with the exception of when we were called back to the unit for count. Life in Level Two made me feel like I was actually getting close to freedom, but I also felt nervous. The new wing of the prison was full of newer inmates who were fresh off the street and hadn't yet learned how to jail, and officers who thought nothing of sabotaging our freedom. I had grown mentally since my short stint at Muskegon, but I was apprehensive about whether those changes would stick.

Two weeks after being moved to Level Two, I was transferred to Riverside Correctional Facility, the first prison I had been sent to, back in 1991. Things had changed since I was last there. At the beginning of my incarceration, Riverside had been considered one of the more open and relaxed prisons, but now it was very restricted and run-down.

Coming back made me realize just how much of the prison way of doing things I needed to purge from my system. I had to keep learning how to navigate around potential conflicts, and I cut back on the hustling I had always done to survive. And if I was really going to focus on getting out of prison, I couldn't care about what was going on out on the yard. I understood where the brothers were coming from when they got into beefs with each other, or fought with the guards, but I could no longer let those frustrations get under my skin.

Fortunately, it wasn't long before I settled into the same routine I had followed at previous joints—reading, exercising, and writing down thoughts and story ideas whenever I got the chance. I joined the brothers for Kwanzaa, and I also became a member of the National Lifers Association. Even though I wasn't serving a life sentence, I wanted to use my organizing skills to assist the brothers who were.

I had also gotten classified to take a business computer technology class. That was a no-brainer for me—I knew I needed to learn all that I could about computers in order to pursue my dreams when I came home. I found the class fascinating. Outside of taking data business processing when I was at MR, I hadn't been exposed to new technology. This is one of the costs of being locked up—inmates are basically left behind by the world.

In the evenings, I would work out with the brothers. One day while working out, I met a guy named Anthony Moorer who knew a lot about urban literature and had started a publishing company on the outside. Anthony gave me a lot of pointers. He told me that if I saved up enough money, I could hire an editor and a graphic designer to publish the books I had written. He and I would walk to chow every day, talking about the future and how we would work together in the publishing business when we were released. Those conversations kept me inspired and motivated.

I had been at Riverside for a month when my father brought my younger sisters, Nakia and Shamica, to see me. It was the first time I had seen the two of them in years. It was amazing sitting across from my sisters, who had been little girls when I was arrested but were now young women. We sat in the visiting room laughing and joking and talking about the future. It was 2006, and I was down to two years before my earliest release date. I could sense that my father was getting excited. We had been through so much together, and it seemed like the worst was behind us.

Having my family visit really meant a lot to me. Their presence gave me hope and increased my desire to get out and live my life in a way that honored their sacrifices over the years. My father had stood firmly by my side, and I was looking forward to showing him that his efforts hadn't been in vain. The countdown to my homecoming was under way, and it couldn't come soon enough.

LATER THAT WEEK, I was sitting on my bunk when the unit officer came with the mail. A letter had arrived from Ebony. I had received HOPE-related correspondence from her before, so I didn't get excited when I saw her name on the envelope. I tossed it on the desk to read later, after my unit returned from chow.

At lunch, Anthony and I talked about the latest trends in the publishing industry and how important it was for us to start our own companies. We broke from chow, and when I got back to the unit, I went to my cell and sat down to read Ebony's letter.

But when I started reading, a smile creased my face. Ebony wasn't writing to discuss official HOPE business. Instead, she had sent me a personal note:

March 20, 2006

Brother Shaka,

I pray this letter finds you in good health and spirits. I have been meaning to write you for some time, but I am so forgetful (despite my youth!). I received a letter the other day from Brother Tone that made me go ahead and write. In his letter, he spoke about the need for conscious female correspondence, and asked me to forward his info to some of the sisters I work with. (I work at an African-centered school.) After reading his letter, I thought about you, probably because I met you both at the same time, and wondered if you felt the

same. I assume you have sisters who you correspond with, but may also want to kick it with a sister of like mind.

Yusef gave me your address. I hope that's okay. I've actually never written anyone about anything other than HOPE business. While I have received countless letters, most of which I didn't have time to reply to, I am committed to corresponding with you, even if I don't reply right away. I've gotten so used to the fast-paced world of technology that I usually communicate via e-mail or text messaging . . . so I will have to slow down a bit so that I can compose a letter.

I realize how important correspondence with family, friends, and supporters are to our brothers' development; this may ultimately make the difference in the choices they make once they return home. Even still, I've been neglectful in writing. Perhaps because I shoulder much weight as an active member, and now secretary, of HOPE. But I must admit that it helps knowing you are one of Yusef's comrades. That personal connection, although not necessary, makes writing consistently that much easier for someone like me who's very busy and forgetful to boot. I also plan to write Yusef's baba as well.

Anyway, I am writing you at work, so I must close this letter. I look forward to building with you.

> In struggle,
> Ebony

The letter was short and noncommittal, but it brought back the intense desire I had felt when I first met Ebony. I knew I had to seize the moment and let her know exactly where I stood. I was at a point in my life where I knew it was going to take a special woman to help me break through the rest of the walls that prison had constructed around my heart. I had seen enough of Ebony to know that she possessed the qualities and the spirit of determination that I was looking for.

Sitting at my typewriter that evening, I wrote as though Ebony were in my presence and we were having a conversation. I told her that I wanted to get to know her—all of her. I didn't want to mislead her into thinking I just wanted a pen pal, so I wrote that I was interested in building a friendship with the hopes of us one day becoming more than friends. It was a bold approach, but she was worth the risk.

When I received a response from Ebony a few days later, I was as excited as a puppy. Her letter was full of thought-provoking inquiries and candid responses to my thoughts and questions, and it made me feel special. I felt like we were sharing more than our thoughts and philosophies on life; it felt like we were opening our souls to each other. I was moved less by the topics than I was by the depth and ease with which our conversation flowed. We discussed food security, revolutionary theory, and community activism. We talked about our dreams, visions, fears, setbacks, insecurities, and hopes for the future.

In the years since, Ebony has teased me for putting some serious mack on her in those first letters we exchanged. But I knew the feeling was mutual. She had a way with words that touched places inside of me that no one had before. She caressed my broken spaces with tender poetry, helped me heal by asking questions that no one had asked me before, and shared her personal frailties and triumphs. Her thoughtfulness was second to none, and I knew without a doubt that I wanted to share my life with her.

After a few letters, I let Ebony know in no uncertain terms that I wanted to see her—this time, for a personal visit. She agreed to drive up for a visit, so I went to the counselor to have her added to my visiting list. Soon after, I was transferred to another joint, but two weeks after I arrived at Lakeland Correctional Facility, Ebony came to visit me. It would be my first time seeing her face-to-face since we'd started corresponding.

When the officers called me for the visit, I had butterflies in my stomach, but they settled down as soon as Ebony entered the visiting room. I took her hand in mine. In the cold, cruel world of prison, I hoped I had finally found someone who could love all of me.

21

LAKELAND CORRECTIONAL FACILITY
Coldwater, Michigan
May 20, 2006

When Ebony and I reached our seats in the visiting room, I noticed that something was different about the woman I had met at Carson City. A tightly wrapped scarf had replaced the long, flowing locks that at one time adorned her head, and her glowing skin was healing from a severe bout of acne. It was a dramatic change in Ebony's appearance. During the time we corresponded, I had formed an image of her in my head, looking forward to seeing her beautiful tresses and radiant smile. But she had cut off her locks, and she wore an uneasy expression on her face as we sat together in the visiting room.

For a brief second, I recalled conversations I had had with other inmates about women who dated prisoners. It's not uncommon for women who are going through physical challenges or who have

SHAKA SENGHOR

self-esteem issues to seek out companionship from men behind bars. In many cases, incarcerated men and women are emotionally vulnerable enough that they'll accept companionship from anyone who reaches out, and it's a widely held notion that some people invest their time in inmates because they are a captive audience— both in the emotional and the literal sense.

But if I had any doubts about Ebony, those doubts were quieted once we started talking. Within moments, I could see that her warm spirit and deep, soulful eyes had remained unchanged. She had an ease about her that allowed us to flow in and out of conversation with the fluidity of a gentle stream. Everything about her spoke to her genuine interest. She asked deep, probing questions and answered my questions with sincerity. Sweetness dripped from every word she spoke.

On that visit, we discussed a wide range of subjects concerning life, love, and relationships. She shared with me her passion for urban gardening and how she believed it was necessary for Black people to have control over their own food supply, and I told her about my love of writing and my goals for life after prison. By the time our visit ended, we had discussed everything from privately owned prisons to the reasons behind the abundance of liquor stores, fast-food restaurants, and inferior grocery stores in predominately Black neighborhoods.

When I had begun my transformation, back in the hole, I thought often about the kind of woman I desired to have in my life. I was changing as a man, and I had different needs than I had when I was a teenager slinging dope in Brightmoor. Now I wanted a woman who would challenge me to be the best I could possibly be. I wanted a woman who would love and nurture me; who had a determined spirit and would stand beside me as I fought the system for my release. I needed a woman who had a profound understanding of what it would take for me to transition back to the community and would be there to support and encourage me. My

214

mind craved the nourishment that Ebony provided, and I could sense the feeling was mutual.

But I also knew the Department of Corrections would test our relationship in ways that would make us think we were crazy for daring to love. The system isn't designed for inmates to cultivate healthy relationships with people on the outside. Families of loved ones are discouraged from visiting by the invasive pat searches and the disrespectful officers who talk to them like they are children. Then there was the reality that while the majority of prisoners come from Detroit and other parts of southern Michigan, the majority of them are sent up north to prisons in rural areas. This makes it close to impossible for loved ones to visit often enough to cultivate a real relationship.

A FEW WEEKS after our first visit, I was transferred from Coldwater to a minimum-security prison in Jackson, less than a hundred miles west of Detroit. Ebony and I were excited when we got the news. It was the first time in my incarceration that I had been at a prison close to home, and the first time I had been to a Level One prison. I felt it was a good sign—one that said I was finally on my way home.

When I arrived at Cooper Street Correctional Facility in Jackson, I sought out a few brothers I knew to get a rundown of the prison. They told me that Cooper Street was designed to transition inmates into the camp system, which is the lowest level of security and allows men to work in the surrounding community. Though it meant I was getting closer to going home, it also meant I could be sent north to a camp in the Upper Peninsula, as many as twelve hours from Detroit. When I broke this news to Ebony, she told me to think positively and focus on staying where I was. There were guys who had found ways to stay at Cooper Street until they saw the parole board, and that gave me a glimmer of hope.

The energy at Cooper Street was different from that of any prison I had been to, because inmates were constantly being released to the outside. It felt good to watch guys I had known from other joints walk out after serving nearly their entire adult life behind bars. When I ran into E Love, a guy I had known from the East Side, he told me that he was going home soon, and my confidence soared. E Love was far from a model prisoner, so if they were letting him go, I figured I stood at least a chance of getting out soon.

Once I had settled into a routine at Cooper Street, Ebony and I had a talk about our visits and phone calls. At the time, phone calls cost nearly eight dollars for fifteen minutes on the line, so we tried to limit how often we talked. But it wasn't easy. When we talked, we had such a good connection that we never wanted to stop. On more than one occasion, we would run up a bill so large that the prison would restrict our calls until Ebony paid it down.

Visits came less frequently, but they were a great supplement because seeing each other in person made us feel connected in a way that couldn't be replaced. Some days, we would spend eight hours sitting and talking to each other. Other times, we would play Scrabble or cards while we laughed and joked together, but there were also days when we would hold hands silently, lost in our own world. One of my favorite things to do on our visits was take pictures together. It provided me with an opportunity to sneak in feels on her booty and get extra kisses, especially when we had a cool cameraman.

Each officer had a different approach to couples kissing. Some would give us a minute or longer if we were really lucky, and others would tell us to stop before we'd even gotten started. Whenever there was an officer who really didn't care, we took full advantage of it. The first time that happened, I experienced the deepest sense of fulfillment I had ever had. It was a sensual experience that superseded any sexual experience I had had in my life. As I held Ebony in my arms and kissed her deeply and passionately, it felt as though our souls were making love. I caressed her tenderly and held her tightly for what felt like forever.

When I look back, my antics remind me of a junior-high student getting his first kiss. Whenever I left from our visits, I would kick back on my bunk and play back every detail of our physical contact. I thought about how Ebony felt in my arms and how sweet her lips had tasted. I was on cloud nine. But no matter how much affection we were able to sneak in, I was always left wanting more.

22

COOPER STREET CORRECTIONAL FACILITY
Jackson, Michigan
June 20, 2006

After a few weeks of visits from Ebony, I had stopped worrying about getting transferred to the camp system. Inmates who had been transferred into Cooper Street after me had already been shipped up north, so I thought I had missed the window when I could be sent on that dreaded trip over the Mackinaw Bridge, which connects the lower part of Michigan to the Upper Peninsula.

You can imagine my shock and disappointment, then, when I was told on the day before my birthday to pack up for a transfer. I was terrified. My relationship with Ebony was young and vulnerable, and I knew we were about to be put to the ultimate test—a test of distance and limited contact that left few romances intact.

It didn't matter which camp I ended up at; they all ranged from six to twelve hours from Detroit, and none of the options would provide us with the ability to see each other every week, like we'd gotten used to doing at Cooper Street. I knew inmates who had been over the bridge for more than two years, so by that point, it was more than possible that I could spend the rest of my incarceration up there.

My fingers felt like lead as I dialed Ebony's number to tell her I was being transferred. Would this be the end of our relationship? I didn't want to dwell on the thought, but it was possible it could be true.

When Ebony answered the phone, the sound of her bubbly, melodic voice made my heart ball up in a knot.

"Baby, they're transferring me to a camp up north," I said with a heavy heart. I struggled my way through the explanation. Part of me was afraid that our relationship was too young to endure the trials we were about to face—after all, my relationship with Brenda had failed to survive the same stress. Another part felt selfish for dragging Ebony into the crazy world of prison life. I wanted to tell her to run. I wanted to protect her from the madness of a system designed to break wills, crush dreams, and uproot the few human connections that managed to spring up in its soil.

When Ebony finally spoke, it was through tears. She told me she had been planning to visit the following day to celebrate my birthday and sing me a birthday song. Her voice cracked a couple of times as she shared her plans, and all I wanted to do was take her in my arms and hug away the hurt. I felt helpless. Silently, I cursed the system and the universe for being so cruel. How could this happen? How could something so beautiful and innocent get destroyed? Didn't the officials at Cooper Street see the way Ebony lifted my spirits each time she walked into the visiting room?

Before we hung up, Ebony had collected herself enough to sing me the most beautiful birthday song I had ever heard, the one she had planned to sing on our visit. Parts of the song were in Kiswahili, and her voice was beautiful, yet powerful and firm, as she moved through the notes. While she sang, I dreamed that the two of us were together on the beaches of Kenya, wading in the water, locked in a firm embrace.

BACK IN MY CELL, an ominous feeling washed over me. Would Ebony really stay by my side? I didn't think so. Except for my dad, the people in my life hadn't stuck around when things got hard. I began thinking as if we had already broken up. I couldn't afford to make myself vulnerable to the pain that was about to enter our relationship, so I tried shutting down my emotions.

The following morning, I was transferred to Camp Manistique. It was my thirty-fourth birthday, and here I was, stuffed on a prison bus for a six-hour drive. I hated every moment of the trip because I knew it meant the end of the best relationship and friendship I had ever experienced.

As soon as I arrived at the camp, I called Ebony to tell her where I had landed. Without hesitation, she told me that she'd be up there that weekend. I was at a loss for words. I expected her to say she'd come up at a later date, once she had the time and the finances to plan a trip, yet she was making the sacrifice to see me as soon as possible. It gave me hope that we might be able to survive the curveball that the system had thrown us.

But a few days later, just as we were preparing to see each other, we were dealt yet another blow. I was being transferred again, this time to a secure Level One at the northern end of the Upper Peninsula. An inmate had recently been killed at another camp by an inmate who was doing a long bid, and with my violent background, the administration was worried that I would do the same. The following week, I was transferred to a prison in Baraga, a nine-hour drive from Detroit.

Months into our relationship, Ebony and I were being tested on every level. But despite my initial fears, Ebony proved to be a woman with great tenacity who refused to be defeated by the system. Within months, she had planned a trip to Baraga and drove up to visit me. She stayed for four days, and we spent every second basking in the glow of each other's presence. I had grown accustomed to fighting the system by myself, but Ebony quickly proved that she had the fierce determination needed to overcome whatever obstacles the system might place in our path.

Nine months later, I got into a conflict with an officer at Baraga over a job. The prison had tried to cut down on its budget by firing a number of inmates from their jobs and making those who were left pick up the slack. But when I was told I would be doing twice the work for the same pay, I asked the officer to show me where in the prison policy it said that he could force me to work two jobs. He couldn't find anything in the policy, so he threatened to write me a misconduct if I refused to do the other job.

I followed the order. It wasn't worth losing ninety days of good time, and besides—I had learned to fight using my mind instead of my hands. As soon as I was done with work that day, I requested to be removed from my assignment and filed a grievance for abuse of authority.

I thought I had won the battle, but the next thing I knew, I was again transferred, this time to Marquette Branch Prison, in the middle of the Upper Peninsula. As soon as I arrived, the officers there placed me in solitary confinement, keeping me there for seven days. They claimed that they didn't feel comfortable with me because of the assault-on-staff case I had caught at Muskegon in 1999.

I couldn't believe this was happening. I had already done more than four years in solitary confinement for that case, and I hadn't caught a misconduct in nearly eight years. I had worked hard to rid myself of the man I had been on that fateful day, yet all these years later, I was still being punished for it.

Ebony and my family had no idea where I had been moved, and I had no way of communicating with them. The prison staff refused to give me any of my property, and I was limited to three showers a week with no outside recreation. I knew right then that this was the old boy network at work. The officers didn't take kindly to me writing a grievance on their partner, and they were making me pay for it. In legal terms, what they did is called double jeopardy, but the prison system has a way of forgetting principles like those.

A week later, I was transferred again. This time, they increased my security level to medium, and I was right back in the midst of the madness I thought I had left. After adjusting to an environment where inmates were on the homestretch of their sentences and wanted to do their remaining time in peace, being in medium security again felt like a nightmare. I was back in a place where stabbings and life sentences were the norm.

When Ebony found out that they had transferred me to a Level Two, she went to work writing and calling the administration in Lansing. In the meantime, I was trying my best to dodge the drama on the yard. The week I arrived, there was a war raging, and several guys had been stabbed over the course of the previous few days. A brother I knew came to me and told me that he had a shank I could use, but that was the last thing I needed at that point in my bit. I told him that I was okay and went to my unit.

SHORTLY AFTER I arrived, Ebony came up for a visit, and we strategized on how to get my security level back down and earn a transfer closer to home. But around that time, my old bunky BX wrote to ask me for a favor. He said that a guy who had molested his son and niece was at the prison I was in, and he wanted me to take care of it.

I was conflicted. I had stopped using violence as a way to solve problems. I had gotten to a point where I was tired of the madness of prison and all of the street codes, and all I wanted to do was move on with my life. But BX was like a brother to me. As I thought about how I would feel if my child was molested, my sense of loyalty kicked in, and I decided to make sure the matter was handled. Within a couple of days, I paid to have another inmate stab the guy in the yard.

I was conflicted about this decision, because even though he had done one of the most reprehensible things in my eyes, a part of me felt like he was worthy of mercy. It was the last act of violence I took part of in prison, and a few weeks later, I was transferred to another secure Level One, in Ojibway, which is so far northwest in the Upper Peninsula that it's in the Central Time Zone.

Ojibway was better known to inmates as "O-stab-a-way" because of all the shankings that took place there. Despite its designation as a Level One, it was run like a Level Two, with a long list of restrictive rules. Many of the inmates there had done long stretches in prison, with more years to go, so they were easily provoked. They had grown up in prison, during the era when stabbings and violence were a regular occurrence. When I arrived, the racial tension between inmates and officers was intense because a white officer had recently allowed a white inmate to stab a Black inmate, causing the prisoners to riot in response.

Unlike most Level One facilities, Ojibway had eight-man cubes and two-man cells, but I was lucky to get a cell with only one bunky, where I would have the space to write and study. Mentally, I was preparing for my parole process and my future on the outside, so the fewer distractions I had, the better. I called

Ebony whenever I could, but it was difficult to talk as much as we wanted, because the unit had limited phone access and the calls were expensive as hell.

I was ten hours away from home, but we did what we could to maintain our visits. Ebony would make the long trek with complete strangers in an effort to cut down on travel expenses. I would find a solid brother whose girl was interested in a visit, and she and Ebony would split the cost of gas and a few nights in a hotel.

Ebony's visits, letters, and phone calls became my lifeline. We grew tremendously as a couple during that time, and on my roughest days, I would keep myself grounded by thinking about the dreams we shared and the future we hoped for.

23

OJIBWAY CORRECTIONAL FACILITY
Ojibway, Michigan
2008

As the months wore on, my anxiety grew. Yes, I was getting closer to seeing the parole board, but my freedom hinged on me completing the Assaultive Offender Program (AOP)—a ten-month-long group therapy class required for all inmates with an assaultive case—and I hadn't been placed in it yet.

The problem was, the waiting list for AOP was longer than my arm. Although I had seen many brothers go to the parole board without completing AOP, I didn't want to put myself in their situation. The board refused to release anyone who hadn't completed the program, yet the state didn't have enough slots to accommodate the number of inmates who were required to complete it.

Ebony and I went to work, making calls and writing letters to get me into AOP, only to be turned down time and time again.

At this rate, we knew that my parole board hearing would probably come before I started the class, let alone completed it, so we decided to begin asking our family, friends, and people from our community to write letters to the parole board on my behalf. I was concerned, but I tried to remain optimistic that the board would see how much I had changed.

A few months into 2008, I was added to the waiting list for AOP and told that I would finally be taking the classes at Ojibway. I was excited to get the news, because I knew that it would bring me one step closer to my release. Then I was dealt a devastating blow: the group had been canceled. Like many of the brothers before me, I would be having my first review in front of the parole board without completing AOP.

AS THE DAY of my parole hearing approached, Ebony and I discussed my strategy for the interview. I knew the changes I had made in my heart and in my life, but I also knew the reputation I had gained during my seventeen years in prison. I had accumulated thirty-six misconducts, caught a case for assaulting an officer, and spent a total of seven years in solitary. I knew that my file did not reflect the man I'd become, but I also knew how unforgiving the system could be.

Upon release, my plan was to go to work immediately mentoring young men and women who were staring down the path I had taken in my youth. In the two years we had been together, Ebony and I had started a publishing company, Drop a Gem Publishing, to print and release our first novel. We had also partnered with HOPE to publish a book for children with incarcerated parents, and my writing was starting to appear in anthology books and national magazines. I had no doubt that I would successfully complete parole if given the chance, and I wanted nothing more than to be let out so I could start making a difference in the lives of others.

As I prepared for the biggest moment of my incarceration, Ebony garnered support on my behalf. People from all walks of life—professors, school directors, bookstore owners, and community activists—wrote letters to the parole board that spoke to the importance of the work I was going to do and offering their assistance for when I got out. My father, my sister Nakia, and my stepbrother, Will, wrote about the growth they had seen in me over the years and the ways in which they would support my transition home.

The day before my first hearing, in August 2008, Ebony drove up for a visit with my father, my stepmother, and my son, Jay. I hadn't seen my son in a few years, so I was excited to see this young man who had grown tall and handsome and seemed to have a firm grasp on what he wanted to do with his life. It was also the first time I had seen my father and stepmother in a while, because the distance had kept them from visiting. When they entered the visiting room, they wrapped me in the tightest hugs. They were the Black family version of a Snuggie, providing me the love and warmth that I needed to survive the long, arduous process that I knew lay ahead.

As we settled in, my father began talking about my freedom and what it meant to him and the family.

"Blood, we need you home," he said. "It's been too long. Your sisters need their brother back and your children need their father."

My eyes welled up with tears. I had not cried deeply in the seventeen years of my incarceration, but I couldn't hold it back any longer. It had taken years for me to realize that no one goes to prison alone; my imprisonment had impacted my family as though they were sitting in the cell with me. I felt the overwhelming pressure to free Ebony and my family from the shackles of my incarceration, and I broke down.

"I know this is what we all have been waiting for," I said through tears, "but I want us to be mindful of all the possibilities. The worst-case scenario is they give me a two-year continuation on my sentence. Which means it would be another two years before I see the board again."

I had served seventeen years by that point, but two more years felt like an eternity.

"No matter what they do, we will never leave your side," my father reassured me. "We will be here to support you until they release you."

His words strengthened and emboldened me with the courage to face the board the following morning. I knew I would have a sleepless night, but it ended up being a night of peaceful contemplation, meditation, and prayer. The time had come for me to face my destiny and finally, after all these years, put prison behind me.

But the state had other things in store for me, things that made me nearly lose my mind.

AS MY FATHER and I entered the small, cramped hearing room the next day, an ominous feeling came over me. The parole board member wasn't in the room physically, but I could feel her negative energy coming through the video conference monitor. As soon as she came on-screen, she frowned, looked down at my file, then looked back up at me with a frown that was even deeper than before.

"Give me your name and number," she said, tipping her head to look back down at the paper.

"James White, number 219184," I said politely.

She looked back up, locked eyes, and asked coldly: "Mr. White, why did you shoot and kill another human being over nothing?" She let the question hang in the air as I tried to explain what had happened all those years ago.

"I felt there was a potential threat to my life," I stated quietly, "because I had been shot some months before."

She wasn't having it. "You know, Mr. White, that's a weak and pitiful excuse for killing someone. You do realize that you killed someone, right?"

"Yes."

She became increasingly combative as she asked me about my incarceration and my plans for after prison.

"I have two books I published and others I've contributed to," I said. "I also plan—"

She interrupted me.

"That's cute that you have books, Mr. White, but it doesn't take away from the fact that you picked up a gun and decided to use it to kill someone."

It was clear that she didn't want to hear anything about the man I had evolved into or the things I had accomplished during the last five years. She cut me off every chance she got. I did my best to present my case with integrity and objectivity, but none of it mattered.

When my part of the interview was finished, she asked my father if he had anything to add. My father started speaking, but soon she cut him off, too. She said she had heard enough and the hearing was over.

"Have a good day, Mr. White," she said. "I am recommending you take AOP before being released. You will get a decision in the mail soon." Then the camera went blank.

As I walked back to the cellblock, I was full of mixed emotions. Part of me had wanted to believe that I had a genuine chance of getting parole, but the more I thought about the way the board member had treated me, the harder it was to see that happening. But when Ebony and I talked later that day, she encouraged me to think positive and stay focused on coming home. I trusted Ebony with my life, and her words were the comfort that I needed.

OVER THE NEXT few weeks, we continued trying to get me placed into AOP, but we kept getting conflicting information from the Department of Psychiatric Services. Just when I was wearing down, though, I was told to pack up because I was being transferred downstate to a prison where I would finally be placed in AOP. The following day, I was shipped back to Gus Harrison Correctional Facility in Adrian. I could barely contain my excitement. It had been a long two years in the Upper Peninsula for Ebony and me, and the town of Adrian was only an hour and a half south of Detroit. The long droughts between our visits were finally over.

When I got to Adrian, I spent most of my time in my cube, writing and studying things I knew I'd need to know when I was released. I kept my interactions limited to a handful of inmates I had known over the years, all of whom were also focused on going home. I also took advantage of unaccredited classes offered by Project Community and the Prison Creative Arts Project (PCAP), both sponsored by the University of Michigan. These classes gave me a creative outlet and inspired me as a writer and an artist.

I still hadn't received a decision back from the parole board, and we were holding out hope that they would give me a deferral instead of flatly denying me until I finished AOP. Under this scenario, I still wouldn't make it home on my earliest release date, but instead of having to wait until my next hearing came around, I would be considered for release as soon as I completed the program.

During this time, I was fortunate to meet and develop some genuine friendships with a group of student volunteers from the University of Michigan, who came in and did workshops once a week. We challenged and encouraged one another as artists, and eventually put on a show for the prison. That was my first time acting and writing for the stage, and I loved it. It was also there that I met an incredible writer and theater instructor, who taught me about acting and how to share my voice in different mediums.

A month or so after I arrived at Adrian, I received a letter from the parole board. *You have been denied parole at this time,* it read, *because it is our belief that you are a threat to society, and therefore, shall not be released.* The letter told me that I had to wait another year before my status could be reconsidered.

It was a letdown, but I had expected as much after leaving the interview. Ebony and I felt that the worst was behind us, and now that I had finally gotten into the AOP class, there was always a chance I could be called back early to see the parole board. In the meantime, I focused all of my energy on completing the requirements of AOP. When we got our date to begin the group, I learned that our group would be led by Dr. Skinner, a therapist who had a reputation for kicking people out of the class for trivial matters. Some guys said Skinner held racist beliefs.

I was worried. The last thing I needed was to be kicked out of the class I had waited so long to get into. But from the first day of group, I began to see that the rumors about him were unfair. He didn't go out of his way to be harsh. He was a straight shooter who cared about accountability and wanted us to take all excuses off of the table. He came across as brash and insensitive, but I agreed with his methods. I was tired of listening to guys rationalize the actions from their past.

Things were going great in the group. I was learning a lot more about my cognitive process and the reasons I had failed to handle conflict in the past. I deepened my understanding of empathy and compassion by listening to the stories of the other men who were in the group. Overall I felt like things were going in a positive direction, until one day when Skinner looked me in the eye and said that he didn't think they would ever release me from prison.

His statement came out of the blue, and other inmates jumped to my defense, asking him why he would say such a thing. Skinner replied that it was just his personal opinion based on what he had seen happen to other inmates.

Speaking to the group, he explained, "Shaka not only has a murder case, he also assaulted a corrections officer. I have rarely seen the parole board let anyone out with that kind of record. I think it's going to be a tough battle for him to get out of prison anytime soon." The whole time he was saying this, he had a smirk on his face.

Skinner's words stung, but I was aware of the games he would play to see if he could throw a person off. Instead of expressing anger, I told him that I was confident I would be released at some point and would do something productive with my life. He nodded with a smirk—a smirk that either said he didn't believe me, or he did but would never admit it.

THE MONTHS BEGAN flying by. Ebony came up for a visit every week, sometimes twice a week, and we continued to plan for the future in the faint hope that I would be called back to see the board early. In the meantime, we took advantage of each visit. No matter what the weather was like or how difficult her workweek had been, Ebony faithfully came up to see me, and our bond deepened with each hug, kiss, and conversation.

One day, Ebony came to see me in the middle of a snowstorm. Neither of us knew that the weather would get as bad as it did, or that the back roads leading to the prison would not be plowed until late in the evening. About twenty miles outside of the prison, Ebony got stuck in a ditch on the side of the road. She was stranded in the middle of nowhere with no cell phone reception, and it took about fifteen minutes of sitting in the cold before someone stopped to help her.

When Ebony finally made it to the visiting room, she was visibly shaken, and I felt like a piece of shit. I was tired of seeing her suffer for our love, tired of not being able to do anything about it. Though we never expressed the thought out loud, we both had the same question at the back of our minds:

What if the board continued to deny my parole until I had served my entire forty-year sentence?

24

As AOP began winding down, I was given a date of May 20 for an early parole consideration. It was the date of my father's birthday, and also of my anniversary with Ebony. In my heart, I felt hope stir.

Ebony and I researched the parole board member who was scheduled to interview me. We discovered that she was known to be consistently fair. The weather that day was perfect, too—one more sign of good things to come.

When I entered the hearing room with my father, the energy was different from that of my first interview. This time, the woman from the parole board was in the room with us, and she was upbeat and friendly. After going through the preliminaries, we got down to business.

I started by telling her about my past, using the language I had learned in AOP. I talked about the "thinking errors" I had made in my past, and how I had learned to use "empathetic role-playing" to put myself in other people's shoes and stop reacting from impulse.

I was talking about my journaling habits when, all of a sudden, the board member stopped me mid-sentence.

"Mr. White," she began, "I know they tell you to use all of this language in group therapy, but I'm not interested in that. I want to know who you were at nineteen and what was going on in your mind back then."

Her tone was sincere, but it didn't make the question any easier to answer. I took a moment to gather my thoughts, then began telling her how I had felt when I got shot at the age of seventeen. I told her that I had reacted to that experience by carrying a gun every day, and that I was deeply sorry for having taken my victim's life. I explained the work I had been doing to help other inmates and the mentoring work I planned to do when I got out.

"I'm impressed," she said when I was finally finished. "I've never encountered an inmate who's so prepared for life after prison." She told me that she admired my honesty and the responsibility I had taken for my actions. We wrapped up the interview, and she said I would hear something from the board within the next few weeks.

WHEN I LEFT the interview, I was on cloud nine. I couldn't wait to talk to Ebony and share how the hearing had gone. Ebony came up to see me that afternoon, and we basked in the excitement of the moment as though we already had the decision in hand.

Over the next few weeks, we started planning my homecoming

and making a to-do list of things we needed to take care of before I came home. First on our agenda was finding me employment, because the bookstore where I was planning to work had been forced to close. We talked about the clothes I would need and the paperwork I'd have to fill out to get an ID. The world of normal living felt close enough to taste.

Whenever Ebony came to see me during those few weeks, there was a glow to her that I hadn't seen in a while. When she entered the building, she seemed to light up the room. She was truly my joy, my rock, and I wanted nothing more than to make her the happiest woman in the world.

Every week, I asked my counselor if she had gotten word from the parole board. Each time, she told me she hadn't. She believed, however, that I would be released, because the state was in a budget crunch and they had to start letting more guys go home. The way she saw it, how could they deny me considering how much I had accomplished?

All of this positive energy had me way more excited than I could ever remember being in prison. I couldn't sleep, and when the yard was open, I walked the track nonstop with my homeboy Terry, who was also preparing to go home. We went back and forth, detailing everything each of us planned to do when we were released. I couldn't wait to get out, sell books, and talk to young men and women who were living on the edge and needed a lifeline.

About a month or so after I had seen the board, my counselor came to my cube and said she needed to speak with me when count cleared. The expression on her face told me that something was wrong. She was normally upbeat and cheerful, but when I stepped into her office, her expression held a sadness that I hadn't seen before. When I sat down, she took a deep breath and delivered the words I dreaded most.

"They denied your release again."

I couldn't believe the words that tumbled out of her mouth.

I had done everything possible. I had changed the deepest parts of me, kept a clean record for a decade, and completed every last requirement they had asked of me. And after all of this, they had shot me down yet again. Skinner's words began bouncing around in my head like jumping beans: "They're never going to let you out. They're never going to let you out."

My unit was called for chow, but I didn't have an appetite. Just thinking of the smell of the chow hall made me nauseous. Everything about prison seemed impossible now. I felt like I couldn't take another day of it.

I wanted to curl up and die, mostly because I knew how devastating the news would be to my family. I was tired of seeing them get their hopes up only to have them dashed. So I decided right there that I was going to give up trying. I wasn't going to see the parole board again.

I was nearing my breaking point when I called Ebony to tell her about the decision.

"This is so fucked up, Shaka! I hate this fucking system and the dumb-ass games they play," Ebony yelled into the phone. "I'm on my way out the door. I'm coming to see you."

It should've made me feel better to know Ebony would be there soon, but it didn't. I felt like this would be our last visit. I couldn't picture Ebony going through another year of this torture. I had been inside long enough to know that I could do the entire forty years if I had to, but I couldn't do another year knowing that her happiness was hinging on me coming home. Ebony wanted a family of her own, and I wanted her to have that—even if it meant her family wouldn't include me.

As I took my shower, I tried to piece together the words I would use to break up with Ebony. She had invested her everything into our relationship, but she deserved to have a man who was free to share life with her fully, without restrictions. She deserved a partner who could hold her at night, kiss her in the morning, take her out to nice restaurants, and dance with her whenever the mood struck. She deserved a man who could be a father to her children—who would be there to put toys together, fix bikes, and do the things a father is supposed to do. But I could give her none of that.

AS I SAT silently in the visiting room waiting for Ebony, I made peace with my decision. It had been an incredible experience, loving and being loved by her, but we couldn't keep doing this with so much uncertainty about the future. She deserved to be free even if I wasn't.

When I looked up, Ebony was standing on the other side of the security doors. I could feel tears starting to form when she entered the room, and as soon as she reached me and took me into her embrace, I broke down. We held hands, and I spoke to her through sobs of despair. I looked her in her eyes as I told her that I could no longer allow her to suffer alongside me. She stroked my hands tenderly and wiped away my tears, listening intently as I told her that I wasn't going to the parole board again—I was done playing their game.

Ebony held my hand and looked at me. "There is no way in hell you are giving up and letting them win," she said. Her voice rose as she continued. "We are in it to win it. I will never give up on you. Giving up is not an option, Shaka."

She delivered that last sentence with the same fiery conviction that had made me fall in love with her four years before.

And she wasn't done. She reminded me of everything we had gone through, of how we had overcome every obstacle placed in our path. She reminded me of how strong my spirit was to have endured four and a half years straight in solitary confinement, and how I had done the hard emotional work that others had run from. By the time she had finished, I felt as if I could pick up the prison with one hand.

I knew then that our bond was unbreakable. As we sat together at that table in the visiting room, I felt myself taking in the strength I would need to fight for the freedom I had earned.

So we got down to planning our next steps.

25

A few months later, I was transferred back to Cooper Street in
Jackson. I had completed AOP, which meant there was nothing
keeping me downstate anymore, and I was afraid that they were
about to send me back to the Upper Peninsula. But when I spoke
to my counselor, I was relieved to hear her say she was sure they
weren't going to send me up north to a camp. (In fact, because the
camps up north didn't like taking inmates with violent histories,
she had no idea why I had been sent up there in the first place.)

I spent my days working out with my brother-in-law Smiley
(who had gotten locked up four years earlier) and my guy Derek
Ford. I shared with them the books I had written, and they told
me how much they loved my writing and how proud they were of
me. They were positive lights, and they told me that they believed

243

I would be getting called back early to see the parole board. This time, they said, I would finally be released.

Ebony and I spent as much time as we could on visits and talking over the phone. We kept dreaming of our future together and created vision boards with pictures of her and me in front of our home in Detroit. Ebony even went out and shopped for my coming-home outfit and started preparing the house for my release.

A few months later, I was called back early to see the parole board for the third time. It had been nearly two years since the first interview, and I felt like this was the shot I had been waiting for. Once again, my father accompanied me to the board, and this time, I was being interviewed by a board member who was an older Black gentleman, known for his toughness and no-nonsense approach.

After the preliminaries, he asked me what I would do if I were released. I felt like I was giving the speech of my life.

"If I am released from prison," I said, "I plan to work and volunteer at local high schools and community centers. My ultimate goal is to pursue a career as a writer. I have published a novel and copublished a children's book. I have also been featured in several national publications. But none of those things are what I care about most. Most importantly, I want to get out so I can be a father to my children and an asset to my community."

"What if your plan doesn't work, Mr. White?" he said, peering over the top of his glasses. "And what will you do when you encounter your old homies?"

"I will do what is necessary to make my plan work," I said, "including working a regular job until my career takes off."

The board member continued to probe to see if he could punch holes in my plans, but he could find none. The things I planned to do had nothing to do with getting out of prison. That's not what was most important to me anymore—what I cared about most was righting the wrongs of my past.

When I was done talking, he told me how impressed he was with my efforts and wished me luck on my journey in the event I received a parole. He thanked my father for being a positive influence in my life and wished him the best.

When the hearing was over, I said goodbye to my father and went back to my cell. I replayed the interview over in my head, trying to get a sense of what the board member was thinking. I didn't want to get too excited about the possibility of getting a parole, but this time things felt right, so I lay back on my bunk with a smile on my face.

Three weeks later, I received my parole.

26

Detroit, Michigan
June 2010

On June 22, 2010, the day after my thirty-eighth birthday, I walked out of prison a free man.

When I stepped outside and inhaled my first breath of freedom in nineteen years, I felt like a baby taking in air for the first time. The air tickled my lungs, and I smiled from deep within. I was officially a free man, and this time, I would do freedom the right way.

Ebony and Jay were waiting for me in the parking lot of the parole office. The moment I saw Ebony, I took in her beauty like a man dying of thirst taking his first sip of water. On our visits, she had been forced to dress modestly so as not to be denied entry. Now, though, she was more radiant and sexy than I had ever seen her. Her beautiful locks were twisted to the side, and she was wearing a dress that rode dangerously high on her thighs. We were starting a new phase of our journey together, with no more bars to hold us back, no more zealous guards to scrutinize our kisses and hugs, and no more damn prison blues.

I turned to Jay and hugged him for the first time as a free man, then kissed Ebony with everything I had inside of me. Then I turned to a brother named Red Montgomery who had also just been released. He had promised to be the first person I sold a book to when we got out, and he remained true to his word. Ebony had brought copies of my first published novel with her, and right there in the parking lot, I made my first official book sale.

When we finished our transaction, I said goodbye to Red, and Ebony, Jay, and I got in the car to go get something to eat. We had planned on having lunch at a nice restaurant in the suburbs, but when we arrived, the place had closed for the day. So instead of the special meal Ebony had planned, my first meal was a chicken sub from Subway.

I didn't care. It was the best meal of my life.

THOSE FIRST FEW days of my release went by in a blur. On the first day, all of my siblings, cousins, and friends came by my father's house (with the exception of my sister Tamica, who was living in Seattle). My stepmother had made lasagna at my request, and we had a few celebratory drinks as I got caught up on what was going on in the family. I got a chance to meet all of the nieces, nephews, and little cousins who had been born while I was away. My daughter Lakeisha came over with her son, and it was amazing seeing her in person for the first time since she was a baby. She had grown into a beautiful woman, and I was looking forward to getting to know her and my grandson. By the end of the day, I was filled with emotion at the outpouring of love and support from my family.

The festivities carried on into the weekend. My father held a barbeque in my honor, and more family members came over to celebrate my freedom. It felt great catching up with my cousins, my grandmother, and my aunts and uncles. Friends from the old neighborhood on the East Side came by, along with some of my brothers from the joint. The familiarity of their faces warmed my heart and soul, and I drank in every moment, savoring each conversation, hug, and kiss.

From my first hour at home, Ebony pampered, spoiled, and doted on me. She cooked me meals and drove me around Detroit as I got familiar with the city again and basked in the reality of my freedom. I don't think we slept much the first week I was home. We stayed up late, talking and making up for all of the loving we had missed out on. Each moment felt sacred.

AFTER THE EXCITEMENT of coming home died down, I started settling into a routine building our publishing business. The first week home, I spoke at the US Social Forum, which was being held in Detroit, and sold a few books. Ebony took me to a few local bookstores to set up in-store signings, and we prepared ourselves for a busy summer. Each day felt like a new adventure.

I had never owned a legal driver's license, so one of the first items on my to-do list was to take my driving test. Being locked up for so long made it difficult for me to gauge how far or close things were, so I had a hard time adjusting to being behind the wheel. It took me about three months of studying before I was confident enough to take the test, but when I did, I aced it.

I also spent a great deal of time on the BlackBerry that Ebony had purchased for me. My phone was basically glued to my hands as I learned the technology and worked to rebuild my relationships with family and friends.

I HAD HEARD all the stories of wild coming-home parties and ex-cons who had made it big in the 'hood after returning home. But I had also heard about untimely deaths and men who returned to prison only weeks after being released. As much as I wanted to predict how my transition to normal life would go, I knew I couldn't. I had walked into prison a man-child and walked out an adult—at least that's what I thought. What I hadn't accounted for was my arrested development when it came to adult interactions and behaviors in the free world. I had never held down a real job, never had a mortgage, a car payment, insurance bills, or the demands of a mature adult relationship.

Besides, I was returning to a world that was vastly different from the one I had left nineteen years earlier. When I went to prison in 1991, there were no sleek Apple MacBooks or iPhones, and gas was $1.05 a gallon. There were no social networking sites, and people either called and talked to their friends or met them face-to-face instead of texting and e-mailing. I was essentially being tossed headfirst into a new society that had an entirely different way of communicating, and I found myself struggling to catch up.

Beyond these challenges, I was still technically under a criminal sentence, and the terms of parole are nothing to mess around with. One innocent slip, and you can find yourself back in the joint. Though I was free, the system was still in control of a lot of areas in my life. I couldn't hang around anyone who was on parole or had a felony, and Ebony and I had to fight to get approval for us to live together. I couldn't go out to parties with my family and friends, and I couldn't spend time at any place that sold alcohol. I couldn't even be around children playing with water guns.

As the weeks went by, I found myself getting into a groove. I went to my first Tigers game and took my first-ever flight when I was invited to speak at the University of Wisconsin-Platteville. It was an amazing experience, getting onto an airplane for the first time, and I enjoyed every moment of it—even when we hit turbulence halfway through the trip.

Within a few months, I landed a part-time job writing for *The Michigan Citizen*, which I enjoyed immensely. I reviewed CDs and wrote feature-length stories on writers, musicians, and filmmakers in the community. But soon, the paper went through a round of budget cuts, and they were forced to reduce my salary and only give me a few assignments a week. It was too much of a financial strain for me. I had just purchased my first car, a gas-guzzling 1996 Caprice Classic, so by the time I had driven around the city gathering information for a story, I would hardly break even. I was thankful for the experience, but knew that I had to make things happen on my own.

THE YEAR 2011 was a big one for Ebony and me. I had met a local filmmaker who wanted to make a documentary about my life. I also landed my first acting gig, playing a single father named Darren in *The Mocha Monologues*, a production that dramatizes relationship problems that single men and fathers face.

In February of that year, Ebony and I moved into a new town house, and shortly thereafter discovered she was pregnant. It was the greatest news in the world, and the day we found out, we cried with joy. Ebony had long dreamed of being a mommy, and I knew she would be the best mother in the world.

As we celebrated the news with our family and friends, my desire to succeed increased. Until that point, Ebony had been providing most of our income. My book sales were growing, but the profits weren't enough to constitute a real living, and I wanted to relieve Ebony of the financial burden of caring for our family.

I started putting in résumés and seeking out employment, but none of my efforts netted anything. I had applied for a position as a reentry counselor at a local shelter for men who had felonies and substance-abuse issues, and I also applied for several youth counselor positions at various nonprofits—jobs I thought would be perfect for me. But nothing came through. The economy was tough already, and it didn't help that I had the stigma of incarceration clinging to me.

Ebony didn't flinch, though. She kept encouraging me to not give up or give in. Even though I was struggling emotionally and financially, I continued to volunteer with youth in the community, sell my books, and speak at local high schools and colleges. The highlight of this work was having the chance to meet Dr. Cornel West during a return trip to UW-Platteville.

Around this same time, the Knight Foundation rolled out a pilot program called BMe (Black Male Engagement), which recognizes Black men doing positive things in their community, and I was nominated for their leadership award. I created a video profile, and people in my social network promoted it among their friends and family, putting me on the grant-makers' radar. Ebony and I submitted a proposal for a twelve-week mentoring program that would teach at-risk youth to use writing to process their emotions and get at the root of their anger and frustration—an idea I had gotten after seeing two of my nephews and one of my childhood friends get shot the previous summer. My hope was that, with the guidance of a mentor and the self-examination I had discovered through literature, children in our community could begin making sense of their environment and receive the love, acceptance, and guidance that they needed to thrive.

A month after submitting my proposal, I got the news that I was one of the winners of the BMe Challenge. I couldn't wait to implement the project at the schools where I had been mentoring.

BUT THE EXCITEMENT in my professional life was nothing compared to the excitement of knowing we had a baby on the way. With each doctor's visit, our anticipation grew, and we soon learned that we would be having a boy. We chose the name Sekou Akili—which means "scholarly warrior"—and began preparing for our son's entrance into the world. I knew I could never make up for the time I had missed with my two older children, but I was determined to be the best father I could be to Sekou.

Which is not to say that this part of our life didn't come with its challenges. Throughout Ebony's pregnancy, Sekou was snugly nestled sideways in her womb. The doctor warned that if he didn't turn around, he would have to be delivered by cesarean section, a procedure that Ebony dreaded. She wanted to experience natural childbirth, and I was heartbroken because I knew how much it meant to her. We had gone to birthing classes, and we did everything we could to prepare for a natural birth, but Sekou didn't want to cooperate.

During one of our final ultrasounds, three weeks before Sekou's due date, the doctor confirmed that Sekou hadn't turned. She scheduled Ebony for a C-section on December 1, 2011. I tried to do my best to help her see the blessing that was before us, but we couldn't help but feel disappointed.

Then, a week before Ebony was scheduled for the surgery, the doctor discovered that Sekou had miraculously turned around.

On December 12, 2011, we checked into the hospital for Ebony to be induced. For eight hours, I watched my best friend, fiancée, and the mother of my child undergo the extreme pains of labor. I coached and encouraged her the best I could, but I would be lying if I said it didn't hurt to stand by helpless as she suffered. Watching her go through childbirth deepened my love and respect for her more than I'd known was possible.

On December 13, 2011, shortly after midnight, Ebony gave birth to the most beautiful baby in the world. Sekou came out with his eyes wide open—bright and loving from day one. Whenever I would enter the room, a big smile would spread across his face. When I held him, he clung to my finger and snuggled up to me, falling asleep to the sound of my heartbeat.

The first few months were a challenge as we managed the adjustments and exhaustion that all new parents face, but I wouldn't trade those months for anything.

Watching Sekou grow, I realized that the desires I had expressed to the parole board were real—more than anything in the world, my dream was to give our son a better world than the one Ebony and I had inherited. And I also discovered that I couldn't have chosen a better coparent. Ebony's tenderness, thoughtfulness, and motherly instinct kept Sekou covered in a blanket of pure maternal love from the day he was born.

IN EARLY 2012, the BMe Challenge winners were invited to a reception where we would receive our leadership awards. It was a great day for me and my family. Yusef was there, having also won one of the awards, and we talked about how our lives had come full circle from our days at the Michigan Reformatory. But the best part of that day was sharing the experience with my father. For years I had longed to show him that I was serious about changing my life. This award was really a reward for him—for the love and loyalty he had shown me all those years.

Over the course of the next few months, I made trips to Wisconsin and New York, speaking to students and continuing my mentoring work in Detroit. My mentorship project was also in full swing. The students were enjoying the class, and I loved watching these shy, introverted, street-toughened kids blossom into brilliant writers and expressive artists, right before my eyes. There was something profound about listening to them speak without interruption, and with each story, poem, or haiku they shared with me, I found myself learning what it truly means to support someone else in his or her journey. They opened up about stories of sexual and child abuse that were both horrifying and heartrending. But in each line they wrote, I could see a ray of hope shining through.

When May arrived, my focus shifted to walking down my last month of parole. By now, it had been nearly two years since I walked out of prison, and I couldn't wait until June to be able to say that it was finally over. I was fatigued from dealing with all of the parole restrictions, and the fact that my BMe grant was running out meant that I would soon be unemployed—but Ebony and Sekou kept me strong.

Finally, on June 28, 2012, I was released from parole. When I exited the office with discharge papers in hand, I had a bop in my step as I thought about how I would never again have to ask permission to travel out of state, or have to pee in a cup while strange men stared at my penis to ensure that the urine was actually coming from me. For the first time in more than twenty years, I would be able to live my life as a normal human being.

Despite my skill set, finding employment continued to be a challenge in ways that threatened my sanity. I began feeling stressed and depressed. Book sales were nominal and speaking engagements were sporadic. I refused to give up or turn to the streets, but I wasn't sure how much longer I would be able to hold on to the idea of finding a job or making it as an author.

At night, I would talk to Ebony and vent my frustrations. She listened and did her part to encourage me to keep pushing forward. Ebony knew me well enough to know that a nine-to-five would drive me crazy, and she reminded me that it would also affect my mentoring work. I continued putting in résumés, attending networking events, and sitting in on business meetings that I was invited to, but my heart wasn't in it.

THEN, THAT JULY, I was invited to a meeting hosted by the Knight Foundation, where I would meet a group of people who would change my life.

By that time, I was tired of walking into meetings like these with hope and optimism, only to leave feeling uninspired and empty. I had met a few well-meaning people, but they never seemed to follow through on the big plans we had talked about in our conversations and e-mails. They told me that they were interested in working with me and helping me get my life on track, but all it ever turned out to be was empty rhetoric.

This time, the meeting was a presentation by Joi Ito, director of the MIT Media Lab, and Colin Rainey, from the design firm IDEO. They were talking about some development work they wanted to do in Detroit. I had no idea who either of them was, and when I looked at them standing at the front of the room, I was convinced that they were no different from the rest of the outsiders who saw Detroit as a charity case. I figured they would come in and give some syrupy spiel about planting gardens or painting flowers all over run-down buildings to make the natives feel positive about the blight and violence that surrounded them.

But Joi and Colin were different. They talked about how we could use the technology and innovation at the Media Lab's disposal to help create better lighting on Detroit's streets, increase the use of composting for urban gardens, and ensure that citizens knew the quality of the air they were breathing in. These were tangible solutions to real problems our community was facing, and their ideas sounded exciting and heroic.

However, as I listened to their plans, I got the sense that they were based not on actual, firsthand experience, but on the romanticized version of Detroit that often gets sold in media and the public imagination. (It didn't help that the presentation was being held at a fancy art gallery downtown.) Joi and Colin meant well, and their work had so much potential, but I felt like they hadn't understood the real Detroit or recognized the people who were already working feverishly to make a difference in the city. So I decided to speak up. I raised my hand and told them that their ideas sounded great, but if they really wanted their work to make a difference, they needed to include the real Detroit in the conversation.

When the presentation was finished, I approached Joi and Colin and introduced myself. They thanked me for what I had shared during the Q&A, and I told them that if they wanted, I would take them around Detroit and introduce them to some people who were doing amazing work.

Colin and Joi looked at each other and agreed on the spot. They were on their way back to Boston that day, but they said they were down to come back to Detroit, as soon as they got the chance. We shook hands, and when they left, I felt like something special had occurred.

Within fifteen minutes, Joi e-mailed me and told me how much he had enjoyed our meeting. A couple days later, I got an invitation to visit the MIT Media Lab in Boston. I had never been to Boston, so I was excited for the trip. When I got there, I saw a building that looked futuristic, covered in six-story panes of glass, and the work going on inside blew my mind. On the tour, they showed us cars that fold in half to make parking in cities easier, as well as a gadget called Makey Makey that allows you to make music with bananas or anything else you can think to plug into it. I was floored by the innovation I saw and the energy of the people I met while there. When we sat down for dinner that evening, I knew something magical was happening. I wasn't sure what would come of this, but I wanted nothing more than to bring the work Joi and his team were doing to Detroit.

NOT LONG AFTER the meeting in Boston, Colin told me that he was taking a team to Detroit and asked me if I could serve as their tour guide. When the team arrived, I met them at their hotel and could immediately sense that they genuinely wanted to learn about the real Detroit—to see the complexities, contradictions, beauty, and ugliness of our battle-scarred city.

We piled into two cars and headed up Grand River from downtown, driving through several neighborhoods on the West Side. We traveled through Zone 8, the neighborhood where Yusef had grown up gangbanging, and continued west into Rosedale Park, a nearby enclave of upscale, middle-class families. As the team looked at the big, beautiful brick homes lining the streets, I talked about the many contradictions and inequalities in our city. We drove on down Grand River Avenue, and a few blocks west of Rosedale Park, we entered Brightmoor, the neighborhood where I had grown up selling drugs.

Brightmoor had suffered from decades of neglect, earning a reputation for high levels of gun violence and drug trafficking. But it was also an area full of promise and hope. I told Colin and his team that amid the burned-out houses and vast stretches of empty, overgrown lots, artists and entrepreneurs were working to bring life back into the neighborhood. It's also an area where urban gardens are being used to counter the culture of drug trafficking. We got out of the car and walked around to talk with people and hear about their needs and challenges.

As we drove down block after burned-out block in the capital of the Rust Belt, I watched the varied expressions of my passengers through the rearview mirror. Their faces registered emotions ranging from disbelief and sadness to intrigue and hopefulness. In my own heart, I felt a twinge of embarrassment for our city, for the people who call Detroit home—including myself. It felt like I was seeing Detroit objectively for the first time, and it was painful to witness what had happened to my beloved city.

I felt compelled to explain the societal fractures my city had experienced—and the fractures I had experienced through it. But where was I to begin? How could I sum up the story of how a once proud city was torn apart by the crack trade, political corruption, and the steady outflow of the jobs that had once put food on its people's tables? There was no easy answer, no way of neatly describing what it was like to grow up here and have the weight of this city press on your soul. I couldn't put that feeling into words. So instead, I simply said that there was so much hope and potential there, even amid the violence and the disorder. Even amid the pain, fear, and destruction I had experienced and inflicted in these streets, there was still hope. And there still is.

AFTERWORD

Earlier this year, I was rummaging through the footlocker where I store my journals, letters, and legal documents—the same locker that I carried from prison to prison for 19 years. I was looking for my parole papers when I came across a letter I had gotten from the godmother of my victim, nearly six years into my incarceration. It stopped me in my tracks.

The letter, dated July 31, 1997, had arrived during the point of my incarceration when I was torn between old instincts and new possibilities. I wanted to change—but I didn't want it enough. If you had asked the corrections officers around me that day if they held any hope for me, they would have at least hesitated. More likely, they would have laughed.

But not the woman whose family I had shattered by a bullet.

She had hope. She believed that transformation could happen, even for me.

Dear James,

A few days ago, it was the 6th year anniversary of my son's death. I call Chris* my son because he lived with me much of his life. I'm sure you remember him because you are the man who murdered him.

July 28, 1991 was a very difficult day for me and my family. I had spent 3 years being a caregiver for Chris's mother, and she had just died of cancer in December. And then, six months later, I received the phone call that our son, Chris, was dead.

His brother was devastated. To this day, he says he didn't only lose a brother—he lost his best friend.

Chris had a new baby son, only 10 months old. He also had two daughters. One is now in college, and although she is a very bright girl, she is having terrible bouts of depression because her dad is gone. The rest of our family tries to help her, but there is an emptiness in her life that no one else can fill.

What I want you to know, other than these painful things that you have brought upon my family, is that I love you, and I forgive you. How can I do less? Because God loves you, and I am a Christian, so I humbly follow his guidance. His word tells me (in the Bible) that He loves us all, no matter what we have done or how bad we think we are. And we are to love one another no matter the circumstances.

James, you may think your life is a mess, but you are spe-

---

* Out of respect for the victim's family and their privacy, I have changed his name.

cial. And God is able to pick you up and help you to go on. He can clean up your messes, no matter what they are. God can be your best friend. Just approach him as a little child. Crawl up in his lap and let Him love you. He can fill that empty hole down deep inside.

> Sincerely,
> Nancy

The best I could do when I received this letter was take one small step. I wrote back. When Nancy wrote again, we began a correspondence that continued for years. Still, it would be half a decade before the change she hoped for would begin to manifest itself in my life.

And that's the thing about hope. In the moment when you feel it, it can seem foolish or sentimental or disconnected from reality. But hope knows that people change on a timeline that we can't predict. We can never know the power that a word of kindness or an act of forgiveness will have on the person who needs it most.

What I now know is that my life could have had many outcomes; that it didn't need to happen the way it did. I was once an angry, lost teenager holding a community hostage to fear and greed. Thousands of youth are making the same mistakes every day. But we weren't born that way. None of our children are born that way. And when they get that way, they aren't lost for good.

That's why I'm asking you to envision a world where men and women aren't held hostage to their pasts, where misdeeds and mistakes don't define you for the rest of your life. In an era of record incarcerations and a culture of violence, we can learn to love those who no longer love themselves. Together, we can begin to make things right.

ACKNOWLEDGMENTS

Special acknowledgments to my dream team! I am humbled and honored to work with such a diverse group of dope people. Thank you all for helping to make my dream come true.

I'd like to thank my awesome team at CAA: Michelle Kydd Lee, Cait Hoyt, Michelle Weiner, and Darnell Strom. I'd also like to thank the amazing team at Convergent Books, the Crown Publishing Group, and Random House: Tina Constable, publisher; Campbell Wharton, associate publisher; Derek Reed, associate editor (thanks for pushing me); David Kopp, executive editor; Donna Passannante, director of marketing; Carisa Hays, director of publicity; and Jessica Brown, publicist.

I'd also like to thank my crew at MIT Media Lab and IDEO (Joi Ito, Jess Sousa, Colin Raney, Sean Bonner, Lisa Katayama, Stacie Slotnick); my team at BMe (Trabian Shorters, Benjamin Evans, Sarah Bouchereau, and Alex Peay); and my team at #cut50 (Van Jones, my brother from another mother, Jessica Jackson, Matt Haney, and Alex Gudich). I love the work we are doing to change the world.

Thanks also to Reid and Michelle Hoffman for all that you do to make the world a better place and for your continued support of my work.

Special thank you and acknowledgment to Nancy Weaver. Thank you for extending to me grace in the form of forgiveness. For this I am eternally thankful.

Special dedication to my cousin Charles "Chuck" O'Neal. RIP.

I want to acknowledge all of the amazing people I have worked with and been inspired by. The list is much too long to include everyone, so if by some chance I forgot you, trust that I have you on a special list in my heart. Ebony Roberts, James White, Marie White, Alan Neal, Arthur Neal, Tamica Neal, Will Redd III, Vanessa Redd Campbell, Jermaine "Smiley" Campbell, Nakia White, Shamica White, Sherrod Redd, Calvin Evans, Mama Evans, all of my nephews and nieces, Malik Yakini, Clement Fame Brown Jr., Carmen Brown, Yusef Bunchy Shakur, Virgil Taylor, Katrina Storm, Joel Fluent Greene, Toni Jennings, Melissa Deshields, Marcus Little, Shuntez, O'Neal, Jerrel O'Neal, all of the students at Cody High School and Tri County Educational Center.

To all of my guys on lockdown, much love and respect to you.

Peace,
Shaka

Recommended Reading

During my incarceration, these were some of the most meaningful books I read. They inspired me to walk in the light of my potential, to be more compassionate, and to embrace the power of love and kindness.

The Autobiography of Malcolm-X: As Told to Alex Haley by
Malcolm X
I Know Why the Caged Bird Sings by Maya Angelou
Soledad Brother by George Jackson
Assata by Assata Shakur
Cages of Steel, edited by Ward Churchill and J. J. Vander
Wall
Dopefiend by Donald Goines
As a Man Thinketh by James Allen
The Republic by Plato
Angela Davis: An Autobiography by Angela Davis
Segu by Maryse Condé
The Prisoner's Wife by Asha Bandele
Houses of Healing by Robin Casarjian

The following are books that I acquired when I was released from prison. These books have kept me grounded in the work that I do today, and have helped me grow and evolve as a man. Some are deeply enlightening, others are funny and inspiring, but each of them has left a lasting mark on my life.

The New Jim Crow by Michelle Alexander
Rebuild the Dream by Van Jones
How to Be Black by Baratunde Thurston
The Miracle of Mindfulness by Thich Nhat Hanh
Orange Is the New Black by Piper Kerman
Reach, edited by Ben Jealous and Trabian Shorters

About the Author

SHAKA SENGHOR is a writer, mentor, and motivational speaker whose story of redemption has inspired thousands. He is the author of six books, a former Director's Fellow at the MIT Media Lab, and a Community Leadership Fellow with the Kellogg Foundation. He currently serves as the Director of Strategy and Innovation with#cut50, a bipartisan initiative to safely and smartly reduce the U.S. prison population in half by 2025. In addition to serving as a lecturer at the University of Michigan, Shaka speaks regularly at high schools, prisons, churches, and universities around the country. www.shakasenghor.com